HORRIBLE SCIENCE
TEACHERS' RESOURCES

SOUND

D0767356

Nick Arnold • Tony De Saulles

additional material David Tomlinson

AUTHOR
Nick Arnold

ILLUSTRATIONS
Tony De Saulles

ADDITIONAL MATERIAL
David Tomlinson

EDITOR
Charlotte Ronalds

ASSISTANT EDITOR
Roanne Charles

SERIES DESIGNER
Joy Monkhouse

DESIGNER
Catherine Mason

This book contains extracts from *Sounds Dreadful* in the Horrible Science series. Text © 1998, Nick Arnold. Illustrations © 1998, Tony De Saulles. First published by Scholastic Children's Books. Additional text © 2005, David Tomlinson.

Published by Scholastic Ltd
Villiers House
Clarendon Avenue
Leamington Spa
Warwickshire
CV32 5PR

www.scholastic.co.uk

Printed by Bell & Bain Ltd, Glasgow

1 2 3 4 5 6 7 8 9   5 6 7 8 9 0 1 2 3 4

British Library Cataloguing-in-Publication Data
A catalogue record for this book is available from the British Library.

ISBN 0-439-97191-8
ISBN 978-0439-97191-1

TEACHERS' NOTES

Horrible Science Teachers' Resources: Sound is inspired by the Horrible Science book *Sounds Dreadful*. Each photocopiable page takes a weird and wonderful excerpt from the original and expands on it to create a class-based teaching activity, fulfilling both National Curriculum and QCA objectives. The activities can be used individually or in a series as part of your scheme of work.

With an emphasis on research, experimentation and interpreting results, the activities will appeal to anyone even remotely curious about the Horrible world around us!

PART 1:
SOUNDS AROUND US

Page 11: Sounds gallery
Learning objective
To look at words related to sound.
To use expressions of contrast when describing sounds.
To listen with attention to detail.
That sounds are made when objects vibrate but that vibrations are not always directly visible.
That vibrations from sound sources travel through different materials to the ear.

Start this session with the activity on photocopiable page 11. Ask the children what they can hear inside and outside the classroom, encouraging them to listen out for even the smallest sounds. Compare what children in different parts of the room can hear. Focus your class on notating these sounds using shape and colour. (For example, spiky bright shapes for sudden crashes, and so on.) Collect a number of objects that make different sounds, such as a computer keyboard, a retractable pen, a fan and a whistle. Ask the children to describe and notate the sounds. Compare the results and use them for a class sounds gallery.
Answer: b) and possibly
c). Sounds are all around us.
There are loads of everyday sounds that we don't take any notice of: sounds like the neighbour's cat throwing up fur balls, your gran sucking a wine gum, or a sparrow with a bad cough. If there aren't any sounds going on, you can always listen to your own breathing. (If you're not breathing it might be a good idea to see the doctor.)

Page 12: Sounding it out
Learning objective
To make careful observations and to draw conclusions about sounds.
That sounds are made when objects vibrate but that vibrations are not always directly visible.

Before beginning this session, recap any work you may have done about the conventions of newspaper reporting. In your classroom, put up large signs saying 'SILENCE!' and warn the children that for this experiment it is important that they are silent from the moment they enter the room. On a flipchart write down the information that all sounds have been banned. Then write a question asking how the children think this will affect them and the world around them. Encourage the children to come up and write their ideas on a class list. Give the children photocopiable page 12 to plan a newspaper report on a life without sound, and break the silence to hold a group discussion

Page 13: Vile Vibrations
Learning objective
That sounds are made when objects vibrate but that vibrations are not always directly visible.
That sounds can be made by air vibrating.
To listen carefully to sounds made.
To record results in a suitable table.

Start this session by asking the children to place their hands under their jaws and to make a humming sound. Ask them what they can feel with their hands, and explain that this is called a vibration. Invite the children to tell you any other examples they may know of. Use the activity on photocopiable page 13 to introduce the concept that vibrations can be of different magnitude, depending on the force applied to the ruler and the length of ruler hanging off the table. Focus the children on fair testing and ask them to consider what factors can be varied in their experiment. Encourage the children to design their own data tables, asking them the reason for their choice of design.

The difference between your class shouting their heads off during indoor playtime on a wet Wednesday and the fine-tuning of an orchestra mid concerto may not be as much as you think! The sounds of both are made in the same way, if not with the same intention! Here's how… All sounds are produced by something vibrating. This makes the air in contact with that object vibrate too. This vibration passes through the air until it reaches our ears. We call these vibrations 'sound waves'. The vibrating doesn't stop there because *inside* our ears is a drum. It waits patiently to pick up any vibrations from outside. And then it too vibrates. Now we get to the clever bit: it is these vibrations that are converted into electrical impulses that our brains then interpret. Brains sort out these impulses into sounds we like -and those we're not so keen on… That's when you realise the difference between a spot of classical music and

the unmistakable sound of your class vibrating their vocal chords beyond the legal limits!

Page 14: Hear Hear!
Learning objective
To make careful observations.
To use a range of sources, including first-hand experience, to answer questions.
To record results in a suitable table.
Start this session by asking the children to describe their ears and to say how they use them. Use photocopiable page 14 as the starting point for looking 'inside' the ear. The activity reinforces the concept that sound gets fainter as it travels away from its source. Split the class into working groups and ask each group to choose a quiet sound that can be repeated in a fair test. Measure how far each member of the group can travel away from the sound until they can no longer hear it. Ask the children to display their results using methods of their own choice, such as a graph, table or bar chart. Use these results for a class display.
Answer: Not usually. She means the bones in her ear have vibrated and passed on their motion to the 'oval window' covering the entrance to her inner ear. So her answer could have been, 'Yes.' Confused yet?

Pages 15 & 16: Inside your ears 1 & 2
Learning objective
That sounds are made when objects vibrate but that vibrations are not always directly visible.
To make careful observations.
To use a range of sources, including first-hand experience, to answer questions.

Use photocopiable page 15 to start off a discussion of what is going on inside our ears. Recap any work you may have done regarding vibrations and link it to how we hear sound. Use photocopiable page 16 to record any ideas that your class may have about building a model ear, focusing on texture as well as colour. Encourage the children to think about what objects could be used to recreate parts of the ear and to record what sounds are made with each part. Use the finished model for an interactive display, encouraging visitors to learn through touch as well as sight.

Page 17: Blimey, it's Beethoven!
Learning objective
That sounds are produced when objects vibrate.
That vibrations from sound sources require a medium with which to travel to the ear.

Use some of the children's favourite CDs to play a selection of different styles of music, ending with a piece by Beethoven. Explain that Beethoven composed his music and relied on hearing just as the composers of the CDs did. Use photocopiable page 17 to introduce the introduce the idea that as Beethoven's deafness grew worse his compositions relied more on feeling vibrations, as well as hearing sounds. Use the activity on the photocopiable sheet to gather a range of opinions and hypotheses. If a piano is available, invite the children to play a simple tune on the lowest bass keys and watch the strings vibrate as they press the keys.

Answer: b) The twang sounds louder because the sound vibrations pass directly to the inner ear via the bones in your skull. These bones are very good at passing on sound vibrations. Beethoven used a drumstick held in his teeth to feel sound vibrations from a piano in the same way.

Pages 18, 19 & 20: A touch of magic 1, 2 & 3
Learning objective
To think creatively in science in order to establish links between causes and effects.
To explain an application of sound using scientific knowledge and understanding.
That sounds are made when objects vibrate but that vibrations are not always directly visible.

Use the story of Helen Keller to illustrate how our conversations are all based on a sophisticated code made up of sounds. Sounds are made when objects vibrate, and although they can't be seen, vibrations can be felt. Helen thus began to understand that she could make sounds too, by feeling the vibrations in Miss Fuller's throat and copying them in her own throat. In the session, encourage the children to any different languages they know, and draw on any experiences they may have of learning a second language. Set the children the challenge, working in pairs, to create a code that uses vibration and/or touch. Ask the pairs to use

photocopiable page 20 to record their code, and share the results with others in the class.

Page 21: A touch of magic 4
Learning objective
To think creatively in science in order to establish links between causes and effects.
To explain an application of sound using scientific knowledge and understanding.

Use the story of Helen Keller as the basis of a class play or assembly. Focus your class on writing a script that includes scientific explanations of what is going on in the story so that the audience understands how and why Helen was able to communicate. Encourage audience participation, using tambourines and drums to illustrate vibration in use.

Page 22: Superb Sound Waves
Learning objective
That sounds are made when objects vibrate but that vibrations are not always directly visible.
To decide whether results support or do not support predictions and evidence.

Start this session with a bowl filled with water. Position the bowl so that light falls on its surface. Ask children to drip a single drop of water into the bowl and describe what happens to the surface of the water. (The waves are stronger at the centre than at the edge of the bowl, as they move away from the source of the vibration.) Use the children's observations as the basis of an analogy to describe sound waves, alongside the factfile on photocopiable page 22. Use the 'Dare you discover…' activity to explore this further, encouraging your class to record observations for comparison later.

ISN'T THAT JUST BEAUTIFUL

Answer: a) Sound waves from your voice make the cling film and foil vibrate. The moving light pattern on the wall shows these vibrations.

PART 2:
MEASURING SOUND

Page 23: Fantastic Frequency!
Learning objective
To make careful observations.
That sounds are made when objects vibrate but that vibrations are not always directly visible.

Start by stretching a length of thick string or thin rope across the classroom and asking children to gently wave the string up and down. The waves made by the string are like the waves made by sound as it passes through the air. The number of waves per second of a sound is called its frequency. Frequency is measured in hertz. You may like to explain that radio frequencies are also measured in hertz, but point out that these are radio waves and not sound waves.

Page 24: Delightful Doppler!
Learning objective
To explain an application of sound using scientific knowledge and understanding.
To think about what might happen and what evidence to collect.

Use the story on photocopiable page 24 to start a class observation. Encourage the children to design their own thought experiments (imagined rather than practical experiments). These should be as horrible and wacky as possible. For example, they might like to give a scientist a CD player and roll him down a steep hill on a skateboard past a listening point. Ask the children how they would measure the distance and the changes in the sound. Focus your class on fair testing and presenting results, using their observations to prove or disprove Doppler's theory.
Answer: a) Higher-frequency sound waves = higher sounds. If you stand by a busy road and listen to cars going past you can hear the Doppler effect for yourself. Award yourself half a mark if your answer was **c)**. These problems did happen, but not badly enough to spoil the experiment.

Page 25: The speed of sound
Learning objective
To make careful observations.
To consider a wide range of sources.

Begin by talking to the children about Concorde and what made it different from other planes. Encourage the children to research other forms of supersonic travel, explaining that this word means 'faster than sound'. Use photocopiable page 25 to focus the children on how sound can be measured according to speed.

Pages 26, 27 & 28: The sound barrier 1, 2 & 3
Learning objective
To make careful observations.
To consider a wide range of sources.

Use the story on photocopiable pages 26 and 27 to focus your class on the experiments and theories that led humans to break the sound barrier. Encourage the children to use the internet and books to discover more examples of breaking the sound barrier, and to use photocopiable page 28 to record some of their discoveries.

Page 29: Shattering Sounds!
Learning objective
To use words related to sound.
To communicate data in an appropriate and systematic manner.

Start this session by whispering your introduction, then varying this with a 'normal' voice and finally a raised voice. Ask the children to tell you their observations. Introduce the term 'audible' and ask the children to decide where the different levels of sound you made should go on a scale, using the sound line on photocopiable page 29. Explain that the volume of a sound is measured in decibels. Encourage the children to add their own different sounds and compare their findings. Collate all the individual work to create a class 'sound line'.

Page 30: Noisy Nature!
Learning objective
To make careful observations.
To use a range of sources, including first-hand experience, to answer questions.
To use words related to sound

Show your class a series of flashcards with animals on them. Ask the children to identify the sounds that the animals make. If you have time, you can play a form of 'pairs' by matching the noise to the picture. Many CD-ROM encyclopedias include sounds as well as words and pictures. Use photocopiable page 30 to record the children's thoughts about animals and the sounds they make. Encourage them to include unusual and exotic samples.

PART 3:
USING SOUND

Pages 31 & 32: Design your own concert hall 1 & 2
Learning objective
To make careful observations.
That sounds are made when objects vibrate but that vibrations are not always directly visible.
To think creatively in science in order to explain cause and effect.

Ask the children if they have ever been to a concert of any kind. Focus the discussion on how music can sound different from recordings when played live and that concert venues are built for just this purpose. Use the information on photocopiable page 31 to start the children thinking about the logistics of designing

a concert hall. Once completed, display the designs along with step-by-step instructions about how they would be constructed.

Page 33: Sounds Amazing!
Learning objective
To communicate data in an appropriate and systematic manner.
That sounds can be made by air vibrating.

Talk to your class about different formats for listening to sounds, explaining that as technology has advanced there have been many ways of recording and distributing sound. Use the timeline on photocopiable page 33 to establish this progression, asking the children to consider the reasons why one format was seen as 'better' than another.

Page 34: Striking sound effects
Learning objective
To think creatively in science in order to explain cause and effect.

To explain an application of sound using scientific knowledge and understanding.

Start by asking the children to close their eyes and identify a series of sound effects (use a professional CD), and explain that dramas on radio and television use sound effects to enhance their impact. Encourage the children to add their own ideas to photocopiable page 34 and to write a story or short play that includes sound effects for this dramatic purpose.
Answers: 1 e), 2 d), 3 c), 4 b), 5 a)

EASY! BUT THEN I USED TO PLAY THE RECORDER MYSELF

Pages 35, 36 & 37: Our Orchestra 1, 2 & 3
Learning objective
To relate the children's understanding to a variety of musical instruments.
That sounds are made when objects vibrate but that vibrations are not always directly visible.
That vibrations from sound sources require a medium with which to travel to the ear.

Use photocopiable pages 35, 36 and 37 to focus your class on how sounds can be made, how we can notate these sounds and how we can play the same sounds to form a tune. When encouraging notation, explain that this is a form of agreed code, the same as any written language. Show the children formalised musical notation, explaining that you want them to devise their own codes using shape, repetition and/or colour. Encourage the children to experiment with the glass bottles and other instruments according to the sounds they want to achieve.

   Use this work as the basis for a performance, letting your audience know that the composition, instruments and notation are all the children's work.
Answers: 1 b) Bigger musical instruments make a lower noise. When a larger area vibrates, it vibrates more slowly and this makes a lower sound. There's a larger amount of air in the empty bottle so the vibes are of a lower frequency and sound lower. **2 a)** Hitting the bottle makes the water vibrate. There's a smaller amount of water in the nearly empty bottle (gasps of amazement) and so it vibrates faster and sounds higher. If you got **c)** STOP bashing the bottles so hard!

Page 38: Rhythmic Resonance!
Learning objective
To listen closely to sounds.
To make systematic observations.

Use photocopiable page 38 as the basis for a session to encourage the children to record detailed observations about resonance. Compare and discuss different opinions in order to reach a class consensus. Include a shell as part of your class display, inviting visitors to listen to it and record their observations. **Answer: b)** Some of the sound you hear is the rush of warm air rising from your own hot sweaty body. You can't normally hear this, but the resonating shell makes it louder. You can hear similar sounds if you cup your hand and place it over your ear. Doing this helps to block out noises that might distract you. That's why pop stars sometimes put their hands over their earphones when they're singing. It helps them to concentrate on the music coming through their earphones. That's right, it's nothing to do with their terrible singing.

Page 39: Viscious Vocals!
Learning objective
To think creatively in science in order to explain cause and effect.
To explain an application of sound using scientific knowledge and understanding.

Start by playing 'Good Morning Your Majesty' to focus your class on the range of different sounds the human voice can make. (One child says the phrase 'Good Morning Your Majesty' in a disguised voice while another child has their eyes shut and tries to guess who it was who spoke.) Then use the activity on photocopiable page 39 to encourage the children to observe and reflect on how we use our voices.
Answers: 1 b) The tingling is caused by sound vibrations in your throat. That's how your voice starts, with vibrations in your vocal chords. If **c)**, stop throttling yourself. **2 b)** The vocal chords work in the same way. The more they stretch the faster they vibrate. And faster vibes mean higher-pitched sounds.

Page 40: Dreadful body sounds
Learning objective
That sounds are made when objects vibrate but that vibrations are not always directly visible.
To make careful observations.

Start with an outline of a human body, asking the children to write down the sounds that they are familiar with and which part of the body they associate them with. Brace yourself for some seriously disgusting suggestions and surprise your class by accepting these ideas! Challenge them to work in teams to find out how these sounds are made, sharing research as they go.

Answer: c) Doctors can still use this method to check out what's going on inside your chest. If the chest sounds hollow like a drum it means there is air in the space around the lungs (there should be fluid there).

Page 41: Splendid Soundproofing!
Learning objective
That sounds are made when objects vibrate but that vibrations are not always directly visible.
That some materials are effective in preventing vibrations from sound sources to the ear.
To record results in a suitable table.

Start this session by inviting the children to listen to a favourite CD. Ask for a volunteer to wear unplugged headphones, encouraging him or her to describe the effect this has upon the music. Explain that headphones can be used to protect the ears from sound, giving examples of jobs where people are required to wear them (such as a pneumatic-drill operator). Use photocopiable page 41 to start an experiment comparing the relative soundproofing qualities of different materials. Ask the children to consider the best way to present their final findings.

PART 4:
ASSESSMENT AND QUIZ

Pages 42, 43 & 44: Music Masters 1, 2 & 3
Learning objective
To use words relating to sound.
That sounds are made when objects vibrate but that vibrations are not always directly visible.
To understand how to change the pitch and loudness of sounds produced by some vibrating objects.
That vibrations from sound sources require a medium with which to travel to the ear.

Start by explaining to the children that they are going to record their own radio show about sound. Split the class into teams and give each team an aspect of their 'Sound' topic to research, using photocopiable pages 42 and 43 as the starting point. Encourage the children to turn their findings into poems, songs,

sound drama or music with appropriate sound effects. They should rehearse their programmes prior to recording them. Play the tape recordings back to the class, encouraging positive feedback and a onstructive review.

Page 45: Listen up!
Learning objective
That sounds are made when objects vibrate but that vibrations are not always directly visible.
That vibrations from sound sources require a medium with which to travel to the ear.
To understand how to change the pitch and loudness of sounds produced by some vibrating objects.
To consider a wide range of sources.

Use the true or false quiz on photocopiable page 45 as the starting point for further research, using books and the internet, on animal sounds versus human sounds. Encourage the children to work in pairs and to try their true/false questions on others as part of a class quiz.

Answers: 1 FALSE. Larger ears don't help African elephants hear better but they do help them to keep cool. Their big ears allow more blood to flow just under the skin and so lose body heat into the outside air. **2 TRUE.** Lacewing moths have ears on their wings. All insect ears are thin flaps of skin that vibrate in response to sound, just like our eardrums. The vibes trigger nerves to send messages to the insect's tiny little brain. **3 TRUE.** Grasshoppers have ears on their abdomens, that's the rear part of their bodies. Crickets and grasshoppers make sound to attract a mate and use their ears to listen out for others of the same species (type) of insect. **4 FALSE.** Snakes don't have ears. They can't hear noises, but they can sense the vibrations made by anything walking on the ground. Snakes pick up these signals through their jawbones. **5 FALSE.** Frogs don't have ears but they do have eardrums on each side of their heads. Scientists have played different sounds to frogs. They found that frogs are best at picking up

low-frequency sounds – like croaks! **6** TRUE. An owl's face is shaped a bit like a satellite dish. It's brilliant at picking up sounds and bouncing them towards the owl's ear holes at the edge of the 'dish'. **7** TRUE. Then the aardvarks dig the termites up with their paws and lick them up with a long, sticky tongue. Tasteee! **8** TRUE. The bats swoop down and grab the mice. But the mice do have a chance – they can hear the bats' high-pitched calls.

Page 46: Dreadful Animal Sounds Quiz
Learning objective
To listen with attention to detail.
That sounds are made when objects vibrate but that vibrations are not always directly visible.
That vibrations from sound sources require a medium with which to travel to the ear.
To understand how to change the pitch and loudness of sounds produced by some vibrating objects.

Start this session by playing a recording of whale sounds. Ask the children to describe what they can hear, and invite them to identify what the creature might be. Link this to the quiz on photocopiable page 46, encouraging the children to research their own questions for class use or a class 'Animal Sounds' book.
Answers: 1 a) The frog is very tasty (by frog standards that is). It's only screaming to put you off while it hops to safety. **2 c)** The higher note made by the rattle tells you the snake is quite small. A slow rattle means the snake is tired and sluggish. You want to protect your young so you are prepared to fight. (Answer **a)** and you should be ashamed of yourself.) **3 b)** It's a warning. Get ready for a fight! Looks like feathers are going to fly.

Page 47: True or false?
Learning objective
That sounds are made when objects vibrate but that vibrations are not always directly visible.
That vibrations from sound sources require a medium with which to travel to the ear.
To understand how to change the pitch and loudness of sounds produced by some vibrating objects.

Use the questions and answers on photocopiable page 47 for the basis of a 'Call My Bluff' class quiz, where

the children in each opposing team give definitions and answers, only one of which is true. Encourage the children to make the false answers as plausible as possible, and give extra points for particularly convincing 'bluffs'.

Page 48: Could you be a sound scientist?
Learning objective
That sounds are made when objects vibrate but that vibrations are not always directly visible.
That vibrations from sound sources require a medium with which to travel to the ear.
To understand how to change the pitch and loudness of sounds produced by some vibrating objects.

Use photocopiable page 48 as the basis for a session where you focus not only on the answers but the reasons for the answers. Ask the children to imagine what it is like being a research scientist, asking them what they would have done in each situation described to find out the answer. Encourage them to give reasons for their answers wherever they can.
Answers: 1 c) Sad but true. Scientists have found that the ear is most sensitive to sounds at 500–3000Hz – that's the level of a person talking. Of course, you can hear your friends just as clearly as you can hear a teacher. But chatting in science class isn't recommended, or you might get an ear bashing from your teacher. **2 b)** And not only this, for the brain can recognise a sound within one-twentieth of a second. We can recognise a particular sound because we remember hearing it in the past. **3 c)** Yes, the nerves in your brain trigger signals in response to the sounds picked up by your ears. If the sounds are wild and random so are the brain's signals.

NAME _____   DATE _____

SOUNDS GALLERY

- There are sounds all around us – some are so loud that we can't hear anything else, others are so quiet that we can hardly hear them at all.

- Our brains ignore low sounds that are constant and focus on sounds that might be important or a warning...

Bet you never knew!
Human beings also use sounds to communicate – so you knew that already? Well, bet you never knew that human voices can make more different sounds than any other mammal. That's because you can move your tongue and lips in many different ways to form lots of weird and wonderful sounds. Try making a few now...

Dare you discover ... sounds all around you?

What you need:
Yourself
One pair of ears (If you're lucky you may already have these. You should find them attached to the sides of your head.)

What you do:
1 Nothing.
2 Sit very still and listen.

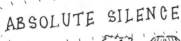

DELIGHTED TEACHER

I SHOULD TRY THIS MORE OFTEN

What did you notice?
a) Nothing. And it gets really boring after the first half hour.
b) I started hearing all kinds of sounds I hadn't noticed before.
c) I heard strange sounds from inside my body.

- **Draw** the sounds that you hear.

- Use shapes and colours to represent the sounds and see if your partner can match the sound to your drawing and identify where in the room it is coming from!

My sounds gallery

NAME _____   DATE _____

Sounding it out

Imagine (if you can) a world without sound. Peace, perfect peace – silence is golden, and all that. You could doze off without ever being woken up, and you'd never have to sit through another science lesson because your teacher would be completely tongue-tied. Sounds perfect? Well, hold on…

A world without sound would also be a dull, lifeless, joyless kind of place. It would be a bit like having to go to school by yourself in the holidays – only far WORSE. Can you imagine it?

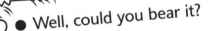

- Well, could you bear it?

- Try to imagine what your life would be like without any sounds at all.

- Write a newspaper report telling your readers what is going on.

- Use the planner to help you.

There'd be no games of football (Can you imagine a totally quiet game?), no chatting on the phone, no one telling jokes, and definitely NO rude noises. There'd be NO FUN. Nothing but a vast, horribly gloomy silence. Sounds dreadful.

THE DAILY BUGLE

Headline

Picture and caption

Subheadings

Quotes

NAME _____ DATE _____

VILE VIBRATIONS

Ruler rackets

What you need:
One 30cm ruler (either wood or plastic)
A table

What you do:
1 Place the ruler half on and half off the table. Hold it in place with one hand on the table.
2 Flick the free end of the ruler with your other hand.
3 You can experiment with different lengths of ruler off the table to make different notes. You'll find that you hear deeper notes when more of the ruler is off the table. Yep, you got it, it's all to do with that larger area vibrating more slowly and making a lower sound.

NAME: Sound

THE BASIC FACTS: What we call "sound" is really a wobbling (called a vibration) of the tiny bits known as molecules in the air. This causes tiny changes in pressure which we detect through our eardrums.

THE HORRIBLE DETAILS: A loud noise like a scream can set off avalanches as the force of the sound dislodges a huge mass of snow. In the winter of 1950–51, avalanches in Switzerland buried over 240 people alive.

COME ON! IT'S THE WRONG TIME OF YEAR FOR AVALANCHES... WHOOPS, SORRY!

● Design a table to record the results of your ruler rackets! Include information about the length of the ruler and the sounds that were made.

OUR RESULTS

My conclusion: _____

_____

NAME _____ DATE _____

Hear Hear!

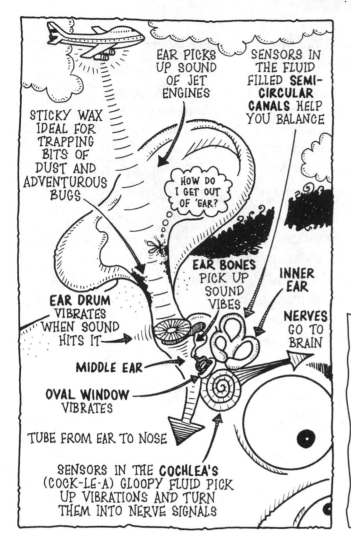

- So that's how sounds get into your head.

- Try this experiment to see just how well your ears work.

- Choose a quiet sound that can be repeated. This is important to have a fair test.

- Now see how far away you can hear the sound from.

- Try it out with all of your group.

- Design a table for your results. You will need to include distance as it's an important part of the data you collected.

Dreadful expressions
Two doctors are at the theatre. But can they hear the play?

Is this painful?

OUR RESULTS

How did you keep the test fair? _____

_____

Inside your ears 1

The ear in action...

Imagine a wandering ugly bug, say a fly, sneaked into the ear. Here's what it would see.

1 The external ear canal (that's ear 'ole to you)

YUCK! STICKY WAX!

ZOOM

2 The ear-drum

RATTLE SHAKE

CRIKEY, A GIANT DRUM! BUZZ

3 Meanwhile, the ear bones in the middle ear are doing their castanets impression by passing on the fly's irritating buzz.

HAMMER ANVIL STIRRUP

BUZZ

ANVIL BONE
STIRRUP BONE
HAMMER BONE

Can you see where the bones' names came from?

4 The semi-circular canals

SLOSH SLOSH SLOSH

BLIMEY!

BUZZ

Scientists use the word 'canal' to mean any long thin space in the body.

5 Cochlea

COCHLEA – HMM, THAT MEANS SNAIL IN LATIN!

BUZZ

That fly's a genius. That's where the name comes from.

6 And the nerves are buzzing with sound messages for the brain.

FIZZ BUZZ FIZZ BUZZ

THIS IS GETTING ON MY NERVES – I'M OUT OF HERE!

NAME _____   DATE _____

Inside your ears 2

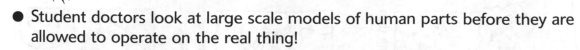

- Student doctors look at large scale models of human parts before they are allowed to operate on the real thing!

- List objects that resemble parts of the human ear.

Ear canal _____

Eardrum _____

Ear bones _____

Semi-circular canals _____

- Use the information on *Hear Hear!* and *Inside your ear 1* to help you make a 3-D model.

- Pay special attention to: colour, texture (sticky waxy texture in some places) and movement (the ear-drums rattle!).

- Horrible health note: Don't pick your ears and use real earwax – it's totally gross!

How to make a 3-D ear: Our step-by-step guide

Things we used:

What we did (use drawings to help!):

Blimey, it's Beethoven!

Ludvig van Beethoven (1770–1827)

Some people called him a genius. Others called him crazy and sometimes even ruder things. His music was inspired by listening to country sounds, murmuring streams, storms and bird calls. He composed thrilling, dramatic melodies that mirrored his passionate feelings about life and art. Hearing had made him what he was.

But in 1800 Beethoven noticed a ringing in his ears and over the next twenty years his hearing failed. He was forced to try a weird variety of different-shaped ear trumpets. The deafness might have been caused by a disease of the bones in Beethoven's middle ear.

He gave his nephew Karl piano lessons and boasted the boy was brilliant. (He must be, thought Beethoven – he had the best teacher in the world.) It was lucky Beethoven couldn't hear the young boy's dreadful playing. Beethoven's deafness made him really miserable. He also began to pong because he rarely bothered to wash or change his clothes. He never brushed his hair. (Don't get any ideas from this – missing a bath doesn't make you a genius.)

THE BOY'S HOPELESS, HE ONLY PLAYS WITH ONE HAND

HE NEEDS THE OTHER ONE TO HOLD HIS NOSE!

PLINK! PLONK!

PONG!

Beethoven could no longer hear well enough to conduct his music. Several concerts were dreadful flops because he conducted the orchestra too slowly.

HE'D DO BETTER AS A BUS CONDUCTOR

SLOW WAVE

But amazingly enough, deafness didn't harm Beethoven's work as a composer. Some experts think he even got better. He used to imagine how the music would sound. And he had a special trick that helped him 'listen' to a piano.

Dare you discover ... how to 'hear' like Beethoven?

What you need:
One 0.5cm wide rubber band
One pair of teeth – preferably your own

What you do:
1 Stretch the rubber band between your fingers and twang it. Note how loud the sound is.
2 Put one end of the band between your teeth. Stretch the band. (Don't let go!) Twang it again.

WARNING
DON'T LET GO OF RUBBER BAND, SUDDENLY!

What did you notice?
a) The twang sounded louder the first time.
b) The twang sounded louder the second time.
c) The twang sounded a higher note the second time.

● Why do you think this is? _____

A touch of magic!

● Helen Keller was born in 1880 and lived to be 88 years old. Her story became famous the world over in books, films and a play. It is an amazing tale of triumph over adversity…

Boston, USA, Spring 1927

The young reporter was in a hurry. He had a deadline to meet and the editor back at *The Daily Globe* office was getting impatient for his story.

"So, Annie, may I call you that? You were Helen's teacher for many years. But what was she really like?"

The old woman smiled weakly. "Well, she was very naughty when she was a young girl. She smashed her mum's plates and stuck her fingers in her dad's food. Then she'd pinch her grandma and chase her from the room."

The reporter raised an eyebrow and stopped scribbling in his notebook.

"So, the famous Helen Keller was a bit of a wild child? Our readers will be shocked."

"Helen couldn't hear or see after an illness that she'd had as a baby. She knew people talked using their lips and she wanted to join in. But she couldn't because she'd

never learnt how to talk. So Helen got cross instead. She drove her parents crazy. Her uncle said she ought to be locked up somewhere."

The old woman took a sip of tea.

"So I bet Helen's parents were pleased when you turned up. You being a teacher of deaf children."

"Yes, they were! They'd written to my boss at the charity in desperation asking him to send someone and I got the job. But Helen was less impressed. I remember our first meeting like it was yesterday. I tried to give her a hug and she struggled like a wild cat."

The reporter tucked his pencil behind his ear.

"So the famous Helen Keller was like a wild cat," he smirked, "Bet you gave her a smack to keep her in line."

The old lady looked shocked. Her saucer rattled as she replaced her cup.

"Oh no, that was never my way. I wanted Helen to be my friend as well as my pupil. Of course, I had to be firm sometimes…"

A touch of magic 2

"Yeah, yeah," broke in the reporter, "but what our readers really want to know is how you taught her. I mean, it's not like she could hear or see anything."

"That was the big problem. All day long I tried to get Helen to understand me by tapping her hand. It was a special code – each letter of the alphabet was a certain number of taps. But Helen didn't understand. It was *so* frustrating."

"Don't suppose it meant anything to her seeing as she didn't know how to read or even what an alphabet was."

"Well, yes I know, but at the time I thought Helen would guess someone was trying to make contact. She'd already made up a few signs herself. Like when she wanted ice cream she'd pretend to shiver."

The reporter was drumming his fingers and fidgeting. "OK, Annie. So you had a problem. How did you get through to Helen in the end?"

"Don't be so fast, young man, I was coming to that. One day we were out for a walk and came across a woman pumping water. Well, I had a brainwave. I put Helen's hand

under the stream, and I spelt out W-A-T-E-R by tapping on her hand. Helen twigged at once and then I knew what to do. I got Helen to feel or taste or smell things. For example, she learnt about the sea by paddling in the waves. Then I told her what they were by tapping. Yes, just like you're doing with your fingers."

The reporter stopped tapping as Annie continued...

"For Helen it was incredible, unbelievable. Just imagine it! You're locked in a totally dark and silent world for seven years, and then suddenly one day you realise that someone is actually trying to make contact with you. Helen changed as if by magic. She stopped being naughty and worked really hard."

The journalist checked his watch. Time was running short. He needed to spice up the story. A new angle.

"But Helen can talk now. What our readers want to know is how you managed to teach her."

"Helen knew things vibrate to make a sound. She could feel my throat move when I talked." Annie put her worn old fingers up to her thin neck. "We brought in a speech expert, Miss Fuller. By touching the teacher's throat and tongue and lips Helen found how they moved. Then she had a go herself. The first words Helen ever said were, 'I feel warm.' Well, she needed ten lessons just to get that far. But Helen stuck at it. And then..."

"You two went all over the world," interrupted the reporter as he buttoned his coat, "and Helen made grand speeches about the needs of people who can't see and hear."

"Yes," the old lady agreed, "and we still live together. Thank goodness for our housekeeper Polly, she looks after Helen most of the time now as I'm getting on a bit. Matter of fact, they're both out in town shopping at the moment."

NAME _____ DATE _____

A touch of magic 3

Hmm, I like that, he thought as he closed his notebook. It would make a great opening line.

- All languages, spoken or signed, are sophisticated codes.

- Work out what your tapping code will be with your partner.

- Write it here to remind you.

Our tapping code

My message:

The reporter stifled a yawn as the old lady continued.

"Mind you, Helen is very capable – despite everything. As I'm sure you've heard, Helen went to university and got a degree. It was all her own work, you know."

The reporter chewed his pencil impatiently. Then he gave a nasty little smile. He scented the new angle.

"It's an amazing story, Annie. But our readers have heard it all before. Devoted teacher helps little girl to discover the world. But maybe there's another side. What do you say to people who claim Helen wasn't that smart and you did the work for her?"

The old lady looked at the young man blankly, then her face filled with anger.

"Well, that's where you're wrong!" she declared fiercely.

"It was Helen who did the learning. Yes, Helen is clever – but that's not the point! You see, I'm blind now myself. Never could see much, in fact. But I've come to realise that even if they can't see or hear, quite ordinary people can still do amazing things. Helen Keller taught me that."

The reporter felt stunned, but his mind was still fixed on the story. "Ordinary people can do amazing things…"

A touch of magic 4

- Use the story of 'A touch of magic' as the basis of your own science drama.

- You will need to split the story into **scenes**, decide what **dialogue** your **characters** should say and think about **stage directions** so that the actors know what to do and where to move.

- Include a team of scientist **narrators** who can demonstrate the science behind this amazing true story.

- Scene 1 has been started for you...

A touch of magic!
Introduction

SCIENTIST 1: Hello and welcome to our brand new production of 'A touch of magic: the true story of Helen Keller'. My associates and I, here in the lab, will help you to understand the science in this amazing story...

SCIENTIST 2: Although we may need your help along the way!

Scene 1: At Helen Keller's house

MRS KELLER: I've written this letter but— *(There is a crash off stage)* Oh no! I hope someone can help us –it's getting so hard!

UNCLE: That girl of yours should be locked up! She's a menace! Throwing things, crying all day, and she's violent – there's hardly a plate left in the house that she hasn't tried to smash to pieces!

MRS KELLER: We know that. That's why I'm writing for help, *(Shows him her letter)*. Look, there's a charity in Boston and I've been told that they can help in cases such as this...

UNCLE: I wouldn't waste my money on the stamp if I were you! It won't make any difference!

MR KELLER *(angrily)*: Don't talk about Helen like that. I know she's been wild lately but it's not her fault. That illness means that she can't see any more and she can't hear. How would you feel? And she's still our precious daughter!

NAME _____   DATE _____

SUPERB SOUND WAVES

Dare you discover ... how to see sound waves?

What you need:
A torch
A large piece of cling film
A cake tin without a base
A large elastic band
Sellotape
A piece of kitchen foil

What you do:
1 Stretch the cling film tightly over one end of the cake tin. Secure the cling film using the elastic band as shown.

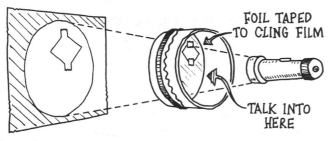

FOIL TAPED TO CLING FILM

TALK INTO HERE

2 Use the sellotape to stick the piece of foil off-centre on the cling film as shown.
3 Darken the room.
4 Place the torch on a table and angle it so the light reflects from the piece of foil on to the wall.
5 Talk into the open end of the cake tin.

What do you notice about the reflection?
a) It jumps around.
b) It stays rock steady.
c) The reflection gets brighter or dimmer depending on how loud your voice is.

NAME: Sound waves

THE BASIC FACTS: A sound wave happens when tiny air molecules are shoved together and bump apart again. As they leap apart some molecules bump into others further away.
   So you get a wave of bumpy molecules moving outwards like the ripples on that pond.

THE DREADFUL DETAILS: It's not safe to stand next to a big bell when it rings. Powerful sound waves from the huge bell at Notre Dame Cathedral in Paris can burst blood vessels in your nose. Some visitors get nasty nose bleeds.

CLING!

NEED A TISSUE?

● Why do you think this is? You can use drawings to help if you like!

_____

_____

_____

_____

_____

_____

NAME _____   DATE _____

FANTASTIC FREQUENCY!

Frequency is measured in Hertz (Hz) – that's vibrations per second. Your amazingly alert ears can pick up low-frequency sounds from about 25 vibrations per second, and they hear up to an ear-smacking 20,000 vibrations every second!

High-frequency sounds include…
• A mouse squeaking

• A human squeaking after seeing the mouse

• A bike chain in need of a drop of oil.

Low-frequency sounds include…
• A bear growling

• Your dad growling in the morning

• Your stomach growling before lunch.

Bet you never knew!
Small things vibrate faster. That's why they make higher frequency sounds than big things. So that's why your voice sounds higher than your dad's, and a violin sounds more squeaky than a double bass.
As you grow up, the vocal chords in your throat that make sounds get bigger. So your voice gets deeper.

● Sort these sounds into two groups. Add some sounds of your own.

| police siren |
| pig grunting |
| cat purring |
| tap dripping |
| scratching down a blackboard |
| *Think of your own* |

low-frequency sounds

high-frequency sounds

NAME _____   DATE _____

DELIGHTFUL DOPPLER!

One of the most amazing sound effects was discovered by an Austrian scientist called Christian Doppler (1803–1853). But in 1835 young Christian was desperate, dejected and departing. He couldn't find a job. So he sold all his belongings and got ready to set off for America.

At the last minute, a letter arrived offering him a job as Professor of Mathematics at Prague University (now in the Czech Republic). This was a stroke of luck because it was here that Doppler discovered what became known as the Doppler effect.

Doppler reckoned that when a moving sound passes it always changes pitch in the same way – that's the Doppler effect. As the sound waves come towards you they're squashed together. So you hear them in quick succession at a higher frequency. As the sound moves away you hear it at a lower frequency because the sound waves are more widely spaced.

To test Doppler's weird idea a Dutch scientist called Christoph Buys Ballot (1817–1890) filled a train carriage with buglers and listened as they whizzed past him. What do you think he heard?

Clue: the test proved Doppler was right.
a) As the buglers came closer the sound grew higher. As they moved away the sound got lower.
b) As the buglers came closer the sound grew lower. As they moved away the sound got higher.
c) The buglers were out of tune and the roar of the train almost drowned them out.

● Design a wacky experiment to test the Doppler for yourself!

● What happens to the sound?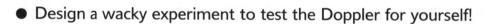

● Draw your observations as a strip cartoon, adding captions if you need them.

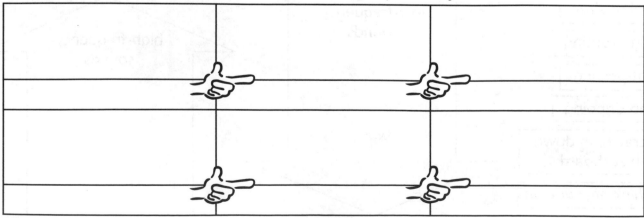

NAME _____

DATE _____

The speed of sound

Have you ever watched a distant firework display? Ever wondered why you see the lovely coloured sparks but don't hear the bangs until a moment or two later?

It proves light travels faster than sound. But how fast does sound travel? A French priest called Marin Mersenne (1588–1648) had a brilliant plan to check it out.

He got a friend to fire a cannon. Marin stood a distance away and timed the gap between the flash when the gun was fired and the bang when the sound waves reached him.

But he didn't have an accurate clock so he counted his heartbeats instead.

In fact, he didn't do too badly. After scientists measured the speed of sound accurately they realized Marin's figure, 450 metres per second was a bit fast. But maybe Marin got excited and his heart speeded up.

One cold day in 1788, two French scientists fired two cannon 18km apart. The second cannon provided a double check on the first and the distance between the two was about as far as each scientist could see with a telescope. They counted the time between the flashes and the bangs.

But what scientists really needed was a bit of posh equipment to make a more accurate measurement. And that's why French scientist Henri Regnault (1810–1878) built this ingenious sound machine. But would it work – or was it just a long shot?

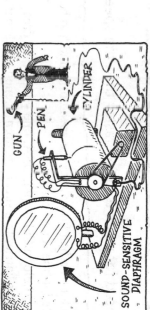

GUN
PEN
CYLINDER
SOUND-SENSITIVE DIAPHRAGM

Here's what happened…

1 The cylinder went round at a regular speed and the pen made a line.

2 The pen was controlled by two electric circuits.

3 When the gun fired the circuit was broken and the pen-line jumped to a new position. I suppose that's what you call 'jumping the gun'. Ha, ha!

4 When the diaphragm picked up the sound, the circuit was restored and the pen flicked back to its original position. Regnault knew how fast the cylinder was turning. So he measured the marks made by the pen and this told him how quickly the test had happened. His measurements proved sound travels at 1220km/h.

● How far can sound travel in half an hour?

Show your
working out
here:

● Design an experiment that could be carried out to measure the speed of sound. Include instructions as well as diagrams.

THE SOUND BARRIER 1

● Scientists raced for years to travel faster than the speed of sound.

By 1947 every pilot who had flown near the speed of sound had been killed. Pilots called it 'the sound barrier'.

But in a secret airfield in California, USA, one young man dreamed of breaking through the barrier in a specially strengthened plane that was designed for high-speed flight. Would tragedy strike again? If one of the project's engineers had kept a secret diary it might have read something like this:

THE SECRET DIARY OF CHUCK YEAGER'S ENGINEER

12 October 1947
Morning

Poor Chuck. What a disaster! He's only fallen off a horse. Bust three ribs — now he can't even move his right arm. I really sympathize with Chuck, but it looks like he's out of the running for the sound barrier attempt. He can't fly a super-fast X-1 plane with only one hand, can he? Chuck looks really miserable. He can be very determined when he wants. Eight "I've been training for months. Eight flights so far — each time a bit faster and this is the big one. It'll take more than a few bust ribs to stop me." he snaps at me.

There's an icy feeling in the pit of my stomach. I think to myself, THIS IS CRAZY.

But I know he'll try it anyway so I figure I'd better help.

Afternoon

The main trouble with Chuck's injuries is that he can't reach far enough to close the X-1's door with his left hand. I poke around in the hanger and find a broomstick. I cut it to size and Chuck manages to close the door using the stick. Don't know how it'll work at 20,000 feet though.

14 October
8.00 am

We're just taking off from the bomber base. The X-1 is slung under the plane we're in. Chuck seems very calm but I can see from his face he's in a lot of pain. "I'm all right," he grimaces. "But I keep thinking about all the pilots who have been killed trying to break the barrier." Well, if that doesn't put him off what will? I wish I could think of something

A few minutes later... This is it. Chuck's climbing down a ladder into the X-1. Now that I've said "Goodbye" to Chuck, I can't help wondering if I'll get a

THE SOUND BARRIER 2

...chance to say "Hi, Chuck" again. My fingers are crossed.

Then I hear the click as the X-1's door locks smoothly. Three cheers for the broomstick handle! But if anything happens to Chuck... it'll be down to that piece of wood and me. I helped him after all.

We can hear Chuck over the radio link with the X-1.

"Brrr, it's cold," he complains.

IT'S COLD!

Well, I'm not surprised. I think. There's hundreds of gallons of liquid oxygen fuel on that plane. It has to be stored at -188°C (-307°F). That's cold enough to frost over the windshield from the inside. Lucky we hit on the shampoo idea. That was a neat trick!

SHAMPOO

① Squirt a layer of shampoo on the glass and it stops the frost from forming

10.50 am

"This is it," says the pilot of our plane nervously. He starts the countdown, "Five... four... three... two... one..."

My heart's in my mouth. Can Chuck really fly the X-1 with just one hand? Should I have stopped him?

"DROP!"

WHOOSH

Too late now he's on his way.

Chuck's got seconds to flick the ignition switch and start the X-1's engines. But if there's a spark near the fuel, the X-1 will be blown to bits. But the engine's firing perfectly.

There she goes! Phew!

"I'm beginning to run," yells Chuck.

But we can't cheer yet.

He's hitting turbulence. Here comes the sound barrier - the next few moments are critical. Will the X-1 fall to pieces like the other planes? The seconds tick away... We hear only silence.

There's a sudden rumble. Is it thunder? No - it's the boom made as Chuck flies faster than sound. He's done it! The X-1's flying smoothly at Mach 1.05! HE'S BROKEN THE SOUND BARRIER! YES, YES, YES!!!

BOOM

WHOOPEE!

2.00 pm

Chuck's glad to be back on solid ground. I'm shattered. Chuck has a huge grin all over his face. He looks on top of the world so I ask him how he's feeling.

"Not so bad!" he laughs.

Not so bad. Not so bad for a guy with three busted ribs!

NAME _____

DATE _____

THE SOUND BARRIER 3

- What breaks the sound barrier? Look for a mixture of man-made and naturally occurring things that travel faster than sound!

picture

My research _____

picture

My research _____

picture

My research _____

WHOOSH

BOOM

NAME _____   DATE _____

Shattering Sounds!

● Here's a chart to compare the loudness of sounds.

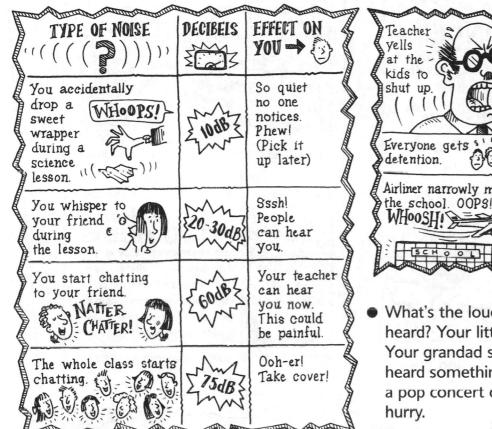

TYPE OF NOISE	DECIBELS	EFFECT ON YOU →
You accidentally drop a sweet wrapper during a science lesson. WHOOPS!	10dB	So quiet no one notices. Phew! (Pick it up later)
You whisper to your friend during the lesson.	20-30dB	Sssh! People can hear you.
You start chatting to your friend. NATTER CHATTER!	60dB	Your teacher can hear you now. This could be painful.
The whole class starts chatting.	75dB	Ooh-er! Take cover!

Teacher yells at the kids to shut up.	90dB	If he yells for too long you could suffer damage to the sensors in your cochlea (inner ear).
Everyone gets detention. SILENCE	0dB	No one dares speak.
Airliner narrowly misses the school. OOPS! WHOOSH! SCHOOL	130dB	Yow! Your ear-drums feel like they might burst.

● What's the loudest sound you've ever heard? Your little brother/sister bawling? Your grandad snoring? Or maybe you've heard something REALLY NOISY. Like a pop concert or a high-speed train in a hurry.

● Draw or list your noise collection along this sound scale.

Quiet   Audible   Clear

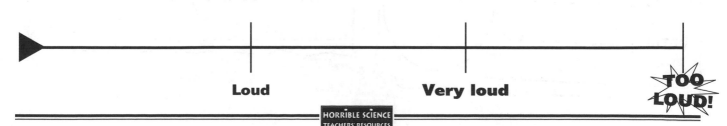

Loud   **Very loud**   **TOO LOUD!**

NAME _____ DATE _____

NOISY NATURE!

The first ever
ANIMAL CONCERT
Live from the Heart of the Jungle
(Sponsored by Bert's Pet Shop)

➤ THE CHOIR ➤

The fantastic FROG male voice choir

CROAK! CROAK! CROAK! *

Delightful loud croaks made louder thanks to vibrating air-filled pouches in their throats. They'll be performing their romantic love song, *"Come here you lady frogs we'd lurve to meet you!"

The rowdy RATS

Famous for their squeaky songs. Some of them perform in ultrasound – that's notes too high-pitched for us to hear. They will be performing their traditional song of welcome to visiting rats,

SQUEAK! SQUEAK! SQUEAK! *

DON'T LIKE THE SOUND OF THIS MUCH

**"Clear off you dirty rats or we'll kill you!"
(The ultrasound version is a bit wasted on humans.)

QUACK! CUCKOO! TWITTER! CHIRRUP! CHIRP! OH DEAR!

The sensational SONG BIRDS

Hear them warble away with their amazing singing syrinxes (see-rinx-es) – that's the skin stretched over their windpipes. (It's the vibrations that make a whistling sound.)

(APOLOGY. The different types of birds are refusing to sing one song and insisting on singing their own tunes all at the same time. This may prove confusing.)

● Research some other animals and the sounds they make.

● Add them to the orchestra!

NAME _____

SOUND _____

DETAILS _____

_____

NAME _____

SOUND _____

DETAILS _____

_____

NAME _____

SOUND _____

DETAILS _____

_____

NAME _____

SOUND _____

DETAILS _____

_____

Design your own concert hall 1

Well CONGRATULATIONS, your school has just been awarded a special grant to build a new concert hall, and you've been asked to lend a hand with the design. Got any ideas? It's important to plan the inside carefully so people can hear music clearly. This is known as acoustics. Fortunately, we've got top DJ Jez Liznin to advise us.

1 The first thing we need is a big tank of water. You can make a ripple and watch it bounce from the walls of the tank.

A TANK HELPS TO PLAN THE WAY THAT SOUND WILL BOUNCE OFF THE WALLS OF THE HALL

PITY IT ISN'T MILK!

2 Now let's look at the walls. Let's go for a curved wall around the back of the stage.

3 Avoid flat, smooth walls in your design. You'll get loads of echoes bouncing around in the wrong places – it'll be like being stuck in a tunnel.

THAT'LL BOUNCE THOSE AWESOME ECHOES INTO THE AUDIENCE!

4 Avoid comfy chairs and carpets and curtains. They'll soak up the sound and make the music sound rather dead. Hard chairs are better for the acoustics even if they do give you a sore bum.

5 Yes, that's right. You've got to build it. Didn't we tell you? Don't work too hard! Byeee!

YO! WAKE UP MAN – YOU'VE GOT WORK TO DO.

HARD CHAIR   COMFY CHAIR

NAME _____   DATE _____

Design your own concert hall 2

My design (drawn to scale 1 : _____)

NEVER GO TO A CONCERT IN A TUNNEL – YOU'LL GET SERIOUSLY BAD VIBES, MAN.

AND HEADACHES

I will need to consider these things in my design:

I will use these materials:

● Now start to make your scale model!

NAME _____   DATE _____

Sounds Amazing!

ONE FINDS
THIS TUNE
FUNKY

- Sound recording has come a long way since Thomas Edison made this amazing invention in 1877!

- Research the sound systems below and see if you can find any others.

- Add them to this timeline in chronological order, along with information you have found.

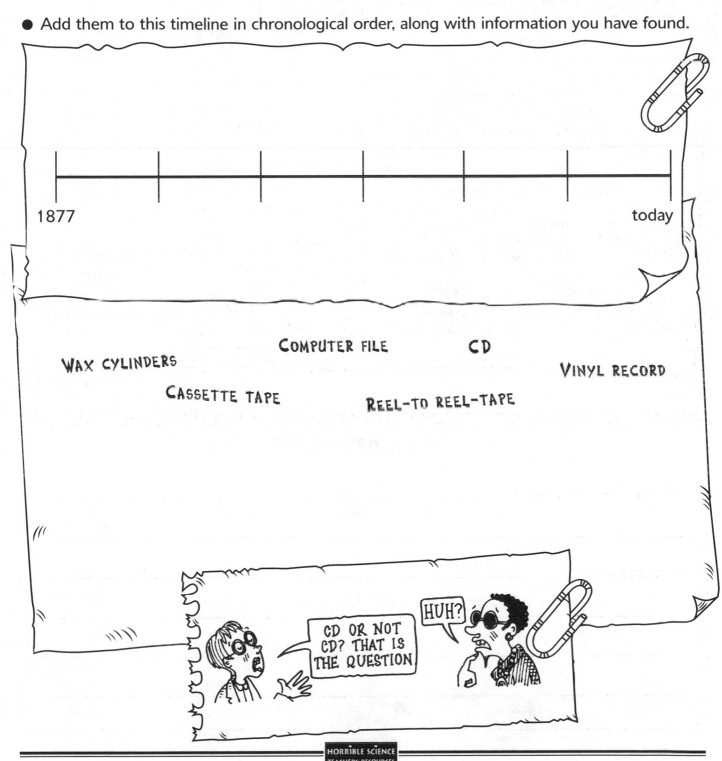

1877   today

COMPUTER FILE   CD

WAX CYLINDERS   VINYL RECORD

CASSETTE TAPE   REEL-TO REEL-TAPE

CD OR NOT
CD? THAT IS
THE QUESTION

HUH?

NAME _____   DATE _____

Striking sound effects

The incredible thing about the human brain is, not only can we hear sounds but we instantly know what they are. We can remember them from the first time we heard them. So you can recognise the curious choking spluttering noise made by a teacher who is just about to lose their temper and dive for cover.

If you listen to a play on the radio you will hear sound effects for things going on in the play. So how sound is your judgement? Can you match the sound effect to the way it's produced? You won't be disqualified for trying the sound effects out. Try recording them on tape, and then play them back with the volume turned up.

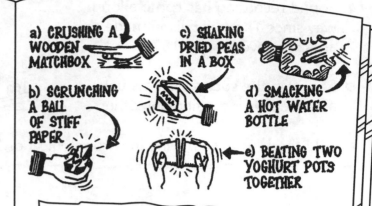

a) CRUSHING A WOODEN MATCHBOX
b) SCRUNCHING A BALL OF STIFF PAPER
c) SHAKING DRIED PEAS IN A BOX
d) SMACKING A HOT WATER BOTTLE
e) BEATING TWO YOGHURT POTS TOGETHER

1 A GALLOPING HORSE
2 A SLAP ROUND THE CHOPS
3 RAIN BEATING ON A ROOF
4 FOOTSTEPS ON A GRAVEL DRIVE
5 A COLLAPSING HOUSE

- Draw an arrow from the sound effect to the sound source.

- Add your own sound effects and try them on your friends to see if they can guess how they are made.

- Now use these effects in a short story of your own. Record your effects so that you can use them when you read out your story. Use the box below to help you to plan it.

MY STORY PLAN

What's the story about? _____

_____

Sound effects: _____

_____

_____

_____

NAME _____ DATE _____

OUR ORCHESTRA 1

Dare you discover … how to play bottles?
What you need:
Three identical bottles
Some water
A spoon

1 All you do is:
1 Fill a bottle with 2.5cm of water.
2 Puff a short breath across its rim. The sound you hear is the air inside vibrating up and down.
3 Half-fill another bottle with water.
4 Puff across its rim as before.

What do you notice?
a) The sound is higher from the nearly empty bottle.
b) The sound is lower from the nearly empty bottle.
c) The sound is much louder in the half empty bottle.

2 Now try this…
What you do:
1 Fill the third bottle three-quarters full with water.
2 Line the bottles up in a row.
3 Tap each one with a spoon.

What do you notice?
a) The sound is higher from the nearly empty bottle.
b) The sound is lower in the nearly empty bottle.
c) When you tap the bottles water splashes everywhere.

● Give each bottle a number or symbol so that you can write down your tune.

● Notate your tune here.

● See if your partner can play your tune!

NAME _____ DATE _____

OUR ORCHESTRA 2

Sonic spoons

Spoons can make some brilliant sounds. The easiest way to do this is to bash two spoons together. This is best done in the privacy of your own home and not in the school canteen. Please note: I did say knock spoons together and not to knock the spoon on…

a) Any nearby priceless ornaments. This could have an effect you'll live to regret.

b) Your teacher's head. The effects of this on you would be too painful to mention.

Super spoon stereo systems

If you want to experience vibrant spoon sounds in stupendous stereo try this high-tech method. Go on, it's dreadfully awesome.

What you need:
Some string
A metal spoon

LIKE THIS!

What you do:
1 Tie some string round the metal spoon as shown.
2 Press the ends of the strings to the opening of your ear holes. Allow the spoon to bang against a tabletop. (No, I don't mean the objects in **a)** and **b)** above.) Incredible sound effect – isn't it? Solid objects like the string are very good at carrying sound waves, remember? That's why you can hear the various sounds made by the vibrating spoon amazingly well.
3 Try holding the spoon by one string whilst tapping it gently with a metal spoon. You could even try playing a tune.
4 Try experimenting with different sized spoons and metal objects such as metal colanders, egg tongs, etc.

● Write a report describing what you discovered.

OUR ORCHESTRA 3

A phantom tweet

What you need:
Half a used matchstick
40cm of thin string
A small cottage cheese carton and lid
A pair of scissors
Sticky tape

What you do:
1 Cut a 1cm wide hole in the side of the carton.
2 Ask for help to make a small hole in the bottom of the carton – just wide enough for the string to go through.
3 Tie one end of the string to the matchstick. Place the matchstick inside the carton and thread the string through the hole in its bottom.
4 Tape the lid in place on the carton.
5 Swing the carton on the string around your head to make a ghostly tweeting sound.

Krazy kazoos
Kazoos make an interesting if slightly weird sound. Here's how to make your own.

What you need:
A piece of greaseproof paper
A comb

What you do:
1 Fold the greaseproof paper round the comb as shown.
2 Press your lips to the side of the kazoo as shown.
3 Here's the tricky bit. Put your lips together so they're only just open and try humming a tune. The air should be blowing out of your mouth and making the paper vibrate.
4 The wacky sound effects are made by the vibrating paper.

Bet you never knew!
A nineteenth-century musician, Mr Curtis, appeared in a concert in Cincinnati, USA. He played an instrument that was like a piano in which the sound was provided by 48 cats. The musician pressed a key

and a cat would yowl as its tail was pulled. But Mr C's cruel plan was far from purrfect. His playing of 'Old Lang Syne' was ruined when the cats all yowled at once. The stage collapsed and someone shouted, "FIRE!" A passing fire engine sprayed the building and everyone got soaked. The cats, of course, escaped by a whisker.

● Try making these instruments.

● Now put your instruments together and play!

NAME _____   DATE _____

Rhythmic Resonance!

Dare you discover … how to make sounds resonate?

What you need:
A sea shell shaped like this…

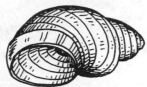

All you do is:
Put it to your ear and listen.
What is causing those eerie sound effects?
a) The ghostly echoes of the sea.
b) It's the sounds around you resonating in the shell.
c) These are faint sounds stored by chemical structures in the shell and released by the heat of your body.

CHECK FIRST THAT NOTHING'S LIVING IN THE SHELL – SORRY, SHOULD HAVE MENTIONED THAT EARLIER

NAME: Resonance

THE BASIC FACTS: Everything has a natural frequency. That's the speed at which it vibrates most easily. When sound waves hit an object with the same natural frequency the object starts vibrating. So the sound gets louder. This is how most musical instruments work.

THE DREADFUL DETAILS: 1 If you sing at a certain pitch the resonance starts your eyeballs vibrating.

2 A trained singer can sing at the natural frequency of a glass and make it vibrate. Some singers can even smash the glass if they sing loudly enough.

WHAT DO YOU THINK?

SMASHING!

LAAH!

● Describe what you hear: _____

_____

_____

_____

● Why do you think this is? _____

_____

_____

_____

VICIOUS VOCALS!

Dare you discover 1 ... how you talk?

What you need:

A voice (preferably your own)

A pair of hands (preferably your own)

What you do:

1 Put your thumb and second finger lightly on your throat so they are touching but not pressing on it.

2 Now start humming.

What do you notice?

a) My throat seems to swell up when I hum

b) I can feel a tingling in my fingers.

c) I can't hum when I'm touching my throat.

Dare you discover 2 ... how your voice changes?

What you need:

A balloon

One pair of hands (you could use the same pair as in experiment one)

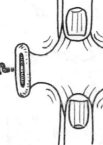

What you do:

1 Blow up the balloon.

2 Let some of the air out. It makes a brilliant farting sound. (No, not during assembly.)

3 Now stretch the neck of the balloon and try again.

What do you notice?

a) No sound comes out.

b) The sound gets higher.

c) The sound gets louder.

NAME: *Your voice*

THE BASIC FACTS: The sound waves of a voice are affected by the shape of its owner's skull and mouth, etc. So every voice is different.

THE DREADFUL DETAILS: People who have had their vocal chords removed can still talk. But their voices come out as a whisper.

Here's where your voice comes from...

ERR!

LARYNX

VOCAL CHORDS

VOCAL CHORDS VIBRATE TO MAKE SOUNDS

TO STOMACH

TO LUNGS

OOOH!

ARGH!

EEEEH!

SOUND ALTERED BY POSITION OF TONGUE, LIPS AND JAWS

Learn how to talk

OK, so you probably know how to do this anyway.

1 Try saying the letters A, E, I, O, U. Notice anything? The sounds are all made by complex air vibrations in your mouth.

2 Now say S, B, P. Notice what happens to your lips and tongue. Can you feel them moving? Can you say these letters without moving your tongue? Thought not.

3 Say N and M. Notice how part of the sound seems to come out of your nose. Try pinching your nose and notice what happens to the sound.

Dreadful body sounds

It's great being you, isn't it? You can make so many smashing noises. Some are musical, some aren't and some are just plain rude. After you make a rude noise have you noticed that that's when your friends make noises, too? Those strange shuddering, tinkling, squeaking, braying sounds we call 'laughter'.

Dreadful burps, farts and raspberries

Here's how to make some entertaining body noises, but **don't** make them…
a) In a science lesson

b) In school assemblies or dinner times
c) When the posh relatives come for lunch.

Otherwise you'll never hear the end of it.

Farting

Made by vibrating skin around your bottom as air rushes out. You can make similar noises by putting your mouth over your arm and blowing hard.

● Now research some other body sounds: whistling, burping, speaking, humming and singing … add your comments and illustrations

Snoring

Made by the uvula (that's the dangling bit at the back of your throat). If a person sleeps on their back with their mouth open, their deep breathing makes the uvula flutter. You can make a disgusting snoring sound by lying in this position and breathing in.

UVULA

Bet you never knew!
So you think your dad/uncle/grandad/pet pot-bellied pig snores like a pneumatic drill? Huh – that's nothing! In 1993, Kare Walkert of Sweden was recorded snoring at 93 dB. That's louder than a really noisy disco. By the way, the best thing to do with someone who snores isn't to hit them over the head. No, all you do is gently close their mouths and turn them on their sides. Ahh, peace, perfect peace!

Dare you discover … how to hear your own chest?
What you need:
Two tupperware boxes with lids (these represent your chest)
Your hands

What you do:
1 Half-fill one box with water and put the lid on.
2 Place the middle finger of your left hand so it's lying flat on the lid of the empty box.
3 Tap the middle portion of this finger with the middle finger of your right hand. The tap should be a smart downwards flick of the wrist.
4 Try to remember the sound.
5 Now repeat steps 1 to 3 on the lid of the box half full of water.

What do you notice?
a) The two sounds are exactly the same.
b) The empty box makes a dull empty sound and the box with water makes a higher sound.
c) The empty box sounds more hollow, the box with water sounds duller.

NAME _____   DATE _____

Splendid Soundproofing!

Here's a lesson in soundproofing from top DJ Jez Liznin and scientist Wanda Wye.

Silent soundproofing

When you record a hit record you don't want to pick up the sound of next door's TV. Jez's sound studio is lined with a thick hi-tech

sound insulator to keep out unwanted noises.

OK, it's only cardboard egg boxes behind plasterboard.

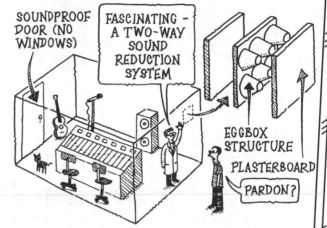

The soft cardboard soaks up the vibes like a nice comfy pillow. And they get lost in there, which is why it's so quiet in the studio. Except when Jez opens his big mouth.

● Some materials allow sound waves to pass through more easily than others.

● Test these materials one by one by wrapping them around a small radio and placing them in a cardboard box.

● How can you make the test fair?

● Which materials reduce the sound most of all?

PAPER BAG   TOWEL

STRING   NETTING

SCHOOL JUMPER   PIECE OF PLAIN PAPER

Think of your own suggestions.

● Why do you think this is?

● Use your findings to create a table of results.

MUSIC MASTERS 1

What do the following have in common?

a) Your pet mouse

b) Your science teacher

c) A sixty-piece orchestra

Give up?

No, the answer *isn't* that they all eat cheese. The correct answer is they all use *sound* to grab your attention. The orchestra needs sound to play a symphony, the mouse needs sound to squeak and your science teacher ... well, just imagine there was no such thing as sound. You couldn't listen to a boring science lesson. And she'd never get to tell you off. That would be tragic!

For animals sound is equally vital because, just like us, animals use sound to pass on vital messages. Just imagine what would happen if your dog couldn't whimper when it was time to go out for 'walkies'. You might forget to take him out...

Speak like a scientist

Scientists have their very own language which only they understand. Now's your chance to learn a few key words. And afterwards you can sound off and amaze your friends and silence your teacher with your word-power.

HIGH AMPLITUDE SOUND WAVES (BIG SOUND = BIG SOUND WAVE)

CHEW-OOO-SCOFF GOBBLE-MUNCH

AMPLE SCIENTIST

AMPLE DINNER

Enormous AMPLITUDE (am-plee-tude)

This means how loud a sound is. Stronger sound waves mean louder sounds, or greater amplitude. The word amplitude comes from 'ample' which also means BIG. Got that?

Fantastic FREQUENCY

Frequency means the number of vibrations a second that make up a sound. These can be incredibly fast. For example, a bat squeak is a fantastic 200,000 vibrations a second. Higher frequency makes the sound higher, which is why bats squeak rather than growl. (Frequency is measured in hertz, Hz). So higher frequency makes more hertz.

Tuneful TONES

No, this has nothing to do with keeping toned by physical exercise. A tone is a sound with just one frequency (just to confuse you, most sounds have lots all mixed up). You can make a tone by hitting a special tool called a tuning fork on a smooth surface.

TUNING FORK

MUSIC TEACHER KEEPING IN TONE IN THE MUSIC ROOM

GARDENING FORK

MUSIC TEACHER KEEPING IN TONE IN THE GARDEN

MUSIC MASTERS 2

Rumbling RESONANCE (rez-o-nance)
This is when vibrations hit an object at a certain frequency. These make the object wobble too. The sound vibrations get stronger and stronger and the sound gets louder and louder. Until it can sound really deafening.

Happenin' HARMONICS
Imagine plucking a guitar string. The string vibrates in several ways to make one tone and several lesser ones. Harmonics are the lesser tones that help to make your playing tuneful. If it isn't, your music teacher is going to get a headache!

● And don't forget the instruments! Jez and Wanda are trying some to start you off.

Drums

It's easy to make a sound on the drums – you just hit them with drumsticks. (No, not chicken drumsticks.)

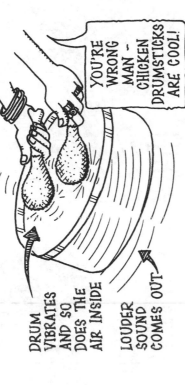

YOU'RE WRONG MAN – CHICKEN DRUMSTICKS ARE COOL!

DRUM VIBRATES AND SO DOES THE AIR INSIDE

LOUDER SOUND COMES OUT

Flute

SPLUTTER!

DRIBBLE!

BLOWING OVER THE HOLE MAKES THE AIR IN THE FLUTE VIBRATE

Saxophone

WHEEZE!

PUFF!

COVERING THE HOLES STOPS THE AIR ESCAPING AND ALTERS THE NOTE

VIBRATING REED MAKES AIR INSIDE THE SAXOPHONE VIBRATE

Guitar

Hmm!

To play the instrument you have to pull, or pluck a string

STRING

VIBRATION FROM THE STRINGS MAKES THE AIR INSIDE THE INSTRUMENT RESONATE. THE RESONANCE PRODUCES SOUND.

NAME _____   DATE _____

MUSIC MASTERS 3

● Things to include in your radio programme:

1 Try your instruments, one by one, telling your listeners what you have learned about the way sounds are made and the way we hear them.

2 Record some of your rehearsals.

3 Interview the composers and technicians as well as the instrumentalists.

● Play your class or group song – good luck!

● One day you'll get to release it on CD! Design your CD cover here.

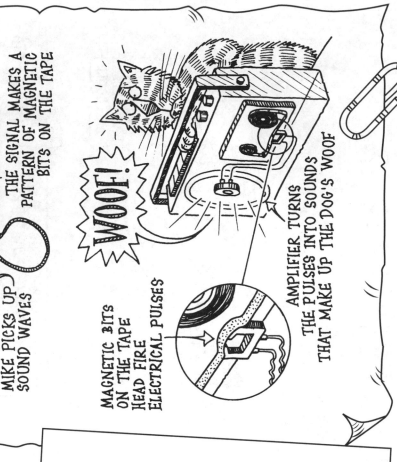

CLASSIC CASSETTE PLAYER

SOUND CAUSES THE RECORDING HEAD TO MAKE A MAGNETIC SIGNAL

THE SIGNAL MAKES A PATTERN OF MAGNETIC BITS ON THE TAPE

WOOF!

MIKE PICKS UP SOUND WAVES

WOOF! WOOF!

MAGNETIC BITS ON THE TAPE HEAD FIRE ELECTRICAL PULSES

AMPLIFIER TURNS THE PULSES INTO SOUNDS THAT MAKE UP THE DOG'S WOOF

NAME _____   DATE _____

Listen up!

1 African elephants (the ones with big floppy ears) can hear better than Indian elephants (the ones with small floppy ears). TRUE/FALSE

I think this is _____

because _____

_____

2 Some moths have ears on their wings. TRUE/FALSE

I think this is _____

because _____

_____

3 Crickets have ears on their legs. TRUE/FALSE

I think this is _____

because _____

_____

4 Snakes have ears hidden under their scales. TRUE/FALSE

I think this is _____

because _____

_____

5 Frogs have ears … er, somewhere. TRUE/FALSE

I think this is _____

because _____

_____

6 An owl's face picks up sound like a large ear. TRUE/FALSE

I think this is _____

because _____

_____

7 Aardvarks have incredible hearing. They can hear termites scuttling about underground. TRUE/FALSE

I think this is _____

because _____

_____

8 Indian false vampire bats (I kid you not – that's what they're called) can hear tiptoeing mice. TRUE/FALSE

I think this is _____

because _____

_____

● How did you do? _____

● Now use books and the internet to help you research questions for an animal and human sounds Horrible Science Quiz!

My questions:

_____

_____

_____

NAME _____   DATE _____

Dreadful Animal Sounds Quiz

Imagine that you are a small animal. What would you do in the following situations? Remember, your choice is a matter of life and death. Choose incorrectly and you might end up as a tasty snack for a larger creature.

1 You're a South American possum – a small furry animal with a grasping tail that lives in

trees) and you meet a Brazilian screaming frog. The frog screams (that's how it got its name, oddly enough). What do you do?

a) Eat the frog. It'll take more than a scary scream to put you off.

b) Run away – the frog is warning you that there's a dangerous animal nearby.

c) Back off. The frog is telling you it's poisonous to eat.

2 You're a North American ground squirrel. There's a rattlesnake in your burrow

and it's after your babies. You can't see the snake but you can hear its sinister rattle. It sounds surprisingly high-pitched and slow. What do you do?

a) Run for it. The rattle warns you that the snake is big and

poisonous. Yikes! The babies can fend for themselves.

b) The slow rattle means the snake is moving slowly. So you've got time to dig an escape tunnel for yourself and your babies.

c) Attack the snake. The rattle proves the snake is smaller than average and rather tired. So you might just win the fight.

3 You're a lapwing (a bird) living in a swamp. You hear a loud three-note call from a redshank (that's another type of bird). What do you do?

a) Go looking for fish. The cry tells you there's food nearby.

b) The call is a warning. There's a gang of crows in the way and they'd like to eat your babies (and the redshank's). You join a posse of other lapwings to fight the invaders off.

c) Nothing. The cry tells you rain's on the way and being a swamp bird you're not scared of a drop of water.

● Make up some questions of your own!

NAME _____   DATE _____

TRUE OR FALSE?

1 You can listen to a concert underwater even if you're at the other end of the swimming pool. TRUE/FALSE

BRAVO! GLUG!

2 You can use sound to count the number of times a fly flaps its wings in a second. TRUE/FALSE

3 You can hear sounds more quickly on a hot day. TRUE/FALSE

4 If you lived in a lead box you wouldn't be able to hear any sounds from the outside. TRUE/FALSE

• Now research some questions of your own and try them on your partner!

Answers: 1 TRUE. Sound travels easily through water. That's why you can hear a rubber band twang even when you hold it underwater. Sound waves pass through water molecules in the same way as air molecules. But the concert would sound muffled because the water would press into your ears and stop your eardrums vibrating normally. (You could make this a trick question and say FALSE because no one can hold their breath that long.) **2 TRUE.** Scientists know the number of vibrations per second for each musical note. All they have to do is to find a note that sounds the same as the beating of a fly's wing. The wing will beat at the same speed. Using this technique scientists have found that a housefly's wings beat 352 times a second. **3 TRUE.** When air is warmer the molecules have more energy and move faster. But sound only travels about 3 per cent faster so you probably won't notice the difference. **4 FALSE.** Sound passes easily through solid metal. But it does pass more slowly through lead compared with steel – 319 km per hour (684 mph), compared to 18,111 km per hour (11,254 mph). But you can still hear the sound clearly.

MY HORRIBLE SCIENCE QUESTIONS

HORRIBLE SCIENCE

NAME _____   DATE _____

Could you be a sound scientist?

● Would you make a good sound scientist? Try to predict the results of these sound experiments. If you get them right you'll certainly have something to shout about.

1 Scientists have discovered that our hearing is sharpest for sounds of a certain frequency. Which sounds do we hear most clearly?
a) Loud music

b) A coin dropping on the floor

c) A teacher talking

I think this is _____

because _____

_____

2 Every musical instrument sounds a bit different even when they play the same note. Some make a smooth tinkling noise and some make more of a rattle or a blare. This is because of the unique pattern of sound vibrations or timbre (tim-bruh) made by each instrument. Scientist Steve McAdams wanted to discover if people could spot these differences. What did he find?
a) People are useless at spotting sound differences. They said all the instruments sounded the same to them.

b) People are brilliant at this. They could tell the difference between the instruments even when Steve used a computer to take out almost all the timbre differences.
c) The experiments had to be stopped when the volunteers developed raging earache.

I think this is _____

because _____

3 A scientist at Harvard Medical School, USA, studied electrical signals in the brain triggered by sounds. What do you think he found?
a) Tuneful sounds trigger wild signals in the brain.
b) All sounds trigger regular patterns of signals.
c) Tuneful sounds trigger regular patterns and dreadful clashing noises trigger wild signals.

I think this is _____

because _____

_____

Bet you never knew!
Diana Deutsch, Professor of Psychology at the University of California, USA, studied the way our ears hear different notes. She played different notes in each ear of a volunteer.

Amazingly, even when she played a high note in the left ear the volunteer said they heard the sound in their right ear. The experiment showed that your right ear "wants" to hear higher notes than the left ear. Sounds weird, doesn't it?

Letts

GCSE
SUCCESS

VISUAL
REVISION
GUIDE

QUESTIONS & ANSWERS

MATHEMATICS
INTERMEDIATE

Author

Fiona C Mapp

CONTENTS

HOMEWORK DIARY

TOPIC	SCORE
Types of Numbers	/38
Positive and Negative Numbers	/25
Fractions	/37
Decimals	/31
Percentages 1	/29
Percentages 2	/30
Fractions, Decimals and Percentages	/30
Approximations and Using a Calculator	/32
Ratio	/24
Indices	/48
Standard Index Form	/34
Algebra 1	/22
Algebra 2	/45
Equations 1	/36
Equations 2 and Inequalities	/35
Number Patterns and Sequences	/27
Straight Line Graphs	/20
Curved Graphs	/20
Interpreting Graphs	/17
Symmetry and Constructions	/22
Angles	/25
Bearings and Scale Drawings	/22
Transformations 1	/22
Transformations 2	/18
Similarity	/22
Loci and Coordinates In 3D	/20
Pythagoras' Theorem	/28
Trigonometry 1	/30
Trigonometry 2	/26
Angle Properties of Circles	/20
Measures and Measurement	/34
Area of 2D Shapes	/30
Volume of 3D Shapes	/29
Collecting Data	/18
Representing Data	/19
Scatter Diagrams and Correlation	/21
Averages 1	/29
Averages 2	/22
Cumulative Frequency Graphs	/25
Probability 1	/28
Probability 2	/25

Planning and revising

- Mathematics should be revised <u>actively</u>. You should be doing <u>more than just reading</u>.

- Find out the dates of your first mathematics examination. Make an examination and revision timetable.

- After completing a topic in school, go through the topic again in the <u>GCSE Success Guide</u>. Copy out the <u>main points</u>, <u>results</u> and <u>formulae</u> into a notebook or use a <u>highlighter</u> to emphasise them.

- Try and write out the <u>key points</u> from <u>memory</u>. Check what you have written and see if there are any differences.

- Revise in short bursts of about <u>30 minutes</u>, followed by a <u>short break</u>.

- Learn <u>facts</u> from your exercise books, notebooks and the <u>Success Guide</u>. <u>Memorise</u> any formula you need to learn.

- Learn with a friend to make it easier and more fun!

- Do the <u>multiple choice</u> and <u>quiz-style</u> questions in this book and check your solutions to see how much you know.

- Once you feel <u>confident</u> that you know the topic, do the <u>GCSE</u>-style questions in this book. <u>Highlight</u> the key words in the question, <u>plan</u> your answer and then go back and <u>check</u> that you have answered the question.

- <u>Make a note</u> of any topics that you do not understand and <u>go back through</u> the notes again.

Different types of questions

- On the <u>GCSE Mathematics papers</u> you will have several types of questions:

  <u>Calculate</u> – In these questions you need to work out the answer. Remember that it is important to show full working out.

  <u>Explain</u> – These questions want you to explain, with a mathematical reason or calculation, what the answer is.

  <u>Show</u> – These questions usually require you to show, with mathematical justification, what the answer is.

  <u>Write down or state</u> – These questions require no explanation or working out.

  <u>Prove</u> – These questions want you to set out a concise logical argument, making the reasons clear.

  <u>Deduce</u> – These questions make use of an earlier answer to establish a result.

On the day

- <u>Follow the instructions</u> on the exam paper. Make sure that you understand what any <u>symbols</u> mean.

- Make sure that you <u>read the question</u> carefully so that you give the answer that an examiner wants.

- Always <u>show your working</u>; you may pick up some marks even if the final answer is wrong.

- Do <u>rough calculations</u> to check your answers and make sure that they are <u>reasonable</u>.

- When carrying out a calculation, <u>do not round the answer until the end</u>, otherwise your final answer will not be as accurate as is needed.

- Lay out your working <u>carefully</u> and <u>concisely</u>. Write down the calculations that you are going to make. You usually get marks for showing a <u>correct method</u>.

- Make your drawings and graphs <u>neat</u> and <u>accurate</u>.

- Know what is on the <u>formula sheet</u> and make sure that you <u>learn</u> those formulas that are not on it.

- If you cannot do a question <u>leave it out</u> and <u>go back</u> to it at the end.

- Keep an eye on the time. Allow enough time to check through your answers.

- If you finish early, check through everything very carefully and try and fill in the gaps.

- Try and write something even if you are not sure about it. Leaving an empty space will score you no marks.

In this book, questions which may be answered with a calculator are marked with 🖩 . All the other questions are intended to be answered without the use of a calculator.

Good luck!

TYPES OF NUMBERS

Choose just one answer, a, b, c or d.

1 What is the positive square root of 81?
 a) 7
 b) −9
 c) 7
 d) 9 (1 mark)

2 What is the reciprocal of $\frac{4}{7}$?
 a) $\frac{7}{4}$
 b) $\frac{4}{7}$
 c) 7
 d) 4 (1 mark)

3 What is the value of 4^3?
 a) 12
 b) 16
 c) 4
 d) 64 (1 mark)

4 Work out the value of $\sqrt[3]{27}$.
 a) 9
 b) 6
 c) 3
 d) 81 (1 mark)

5 Calculate the highest common factor of 18 and 24.
 a) 6
 b) 18
 c) 12
 d) 432 (1 mark)

Score / 5

Answer all parts of the questions.

1 Say whether each statement is true or false.

 a) 2 is the only even prime number. ....

 b) 12 is a factor of 6. ....

 c) 9 is a multiple of 3. ....

 d) 1, 2, 4, 6, 12, 24 are the only factors of 24. .... (4 marks)

2 Work out the answers to these questions.

 a) $\sqrt{4}$ = ... b) $\sqrt{100}$ = ... c) 4^3 = ...

 d) $\sqrt[3]{27}$ = ... e) $\sqrt[3]{-125}$ = ... f) 9^2 = ... (6 marks)

3 Write 72 as a product of its prime factors. .... (2 marks)

4 The number 180 is written as its prime factors. What are the values of a and b?

 $180 = 2^a \times 3^b \times 5$ .... (2 marks)

5 What is the LCM of 20 and 30? .... (1 mark)

6 What is the HCF of 24 and 40? .... (1 mark)

7 Decide whether this statement is true or false.

 $\frac{4}{7}$ is the reciprocal of $1\frac{3}{4}$ .... (1 mark)

Score / 17

C These are GCSE style questions. Answer all parts of the questions. Show your workings (on separate paper if necessary) and include the correct units in your answers.

1 Some numbers are in the cloud below. Choose numbers from the cloud to answer the questions below.

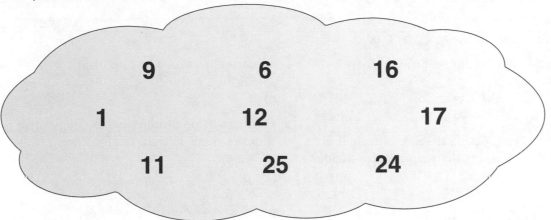

9   6   16

1   12   17

11   25   24

a) Write down any square numbers. .... (1 mark)

b) Write down those numbers which are a factor of 24. .... (2 marks)

c) Write down the prime numbers bigger than 7. .... (1 mark)

d) Write down the reciprocal of $\frac{1}{9}$. .... (1 mark)

2 a) Express the following numbers as products of their prime factors.

i) 56   ....

ii) 60   .... (4 marks)

b) Find the highest common factor of 56 and 60. .... (2 marks)

c) Find the lowest common multiple of 56 and 60. .... (2 marks)

3 The number 360 can be written as $2^a \times 3^b \times 5^c$.

Calculate the values of a, b and c.

....

.... (3 marks)

Score   / 16

How well did you do?
1–11 marks   Try again
12–21 marks   Getting there
22–29 marks   Good work
30–38 marks   Excellent!

TOTAL SCORE   / 38

For more information on this topic see pages 4–5 of your Success Guide.

POSITIVE AND NEGATIVE NUMBERS

A

Choose just one answer, a, b, c or d.

1 Which number is the biggest in this list?
7, 11, −20, −41
a) 7   b) 11
c) −20   d) −41   (1 mark)

2 The temperature outside is −5 °C. Inside it is 28 °C warmer. What is the temperature inside?
a) 17 °C   b) 21 °C
c) 23 °C   d) 25 °C   (1 mark)

3 If these two number cards are multiplied together, what is the answer?   −3   5
a) −15   b) 2
c) 15   d) 8   (1 mark)

4 What is the value of −12 + (−6)?
a) −6   b) −20
c) 6   d) −18   (1 mark)

5 Here are some number cards. Which two number cards add up to give 1?

   −7   4   9   −3

a) −7 and 4   b) 4 and −3
c) 9 and 4   d) −7 and −3   (1 mark)

Score   / 5

B

Answer all parts of the questions.

1 Here are some number cards.   −7   0   5   −3

a) Choose two of the number cards that add up to give −2 ....

b) Choose two of the number cards that subtract to give −4 ....

c) Choose two of the number cards that multiply to give −15 .... (3 marks)

2 Join each of these calculations to the correct answer.

−3 × 4   10

12 ÷ (−2)   −1

−4 − (−3)   −12

−5 × (−2)   4

−20 ÷ (−5)   −6   (5 marks)

3 Work out the answers to the following questions.

a) (−40) ÷ (−4) ....   b) −7 + (−3) ....   c) 8 − (−6) ....   (3 marks)

4 Here are some numbers in a number pyramid. The number in each rectangle is found by adding the two numbers below. Complete the number pyramid.

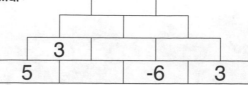

(3 marks)

Score   / 14

These are GCSE style questions. Answer all parts of the questions. Show your workings (on separate paper if necessary) and include the correct units in your answers.

1 The temperature at midnight in various cities on one night in December is shown in the table below.

City	Temperature (°C)
Cairo	4
London	−2
New York	−7
Oslo	−14

a) How many degrees colder is Oslo than Cairo? .... (1 mark)

b) i) On the same day the temperature in Sydney is 24 °C warmer than New York. What is the temperature in Sydney?

.... (2 marks)

ii) How many degrees colder is London than Sydney?

.... (2 marks)

2 One evening last winter, the temperature in Swansea was 4 °C, in Manchester was −2 °C and in Glasgow was −8 °C.

a) Work out the difference in temperature between Swansea and Glasgow.

.... (1 mark)

b) The temperature in Manchester increased by 6 °C. Work out the new temperature in Manchester.

.... (1 mark)

c) The temperature in Glasgow fell by 3 °C. Work out the new temperature in Glasgow.

.... (1 mark)

Score   / 6

How well did you do?

1–6 marks	Try again
7–13 marks	Getting there
14–19 marks	Good work
20–25 marks	Excellent!

TOTAL SCORE   / 25

For more information on this topic see pages 6–7 of your Success Guide.

FRACTIONS

Choose just one answer, a, b, c or d.

1 Which one of these fractions is equivalent to $\frac{5}{9}$?

a) $\frac{16}{27}$

b) $\frac{9}{18}$

c) $\frac{25}{45}$

d) $\frac{21}{36}$ (1 mark)

2 In a class of 24 students, $\frac{3}{8}$ wear glasses. How many students wear glasses?

a) 9

b) 6

c) 3

d) 12 (1 mark)

3 Work out the answer to $\frac{5}{9} - \frac{1}{3}$

a) $\frac{1}{3}$

b) $\frac{2}{9}$

c) $\frac{4}{6}$

d) $\frac{4}{12}$ (1 mark)

4 Work out the answer to $\frac{2}{11} \times \frac{7}{9}$

a) $\frac{14}{11}$ b) $\frac{14}{9}$

c) $\frac{14}{99}$ d) $\frac{2}{99}$ (1 mark)

5 Work out the answer to $\frac{3}{10} \div \frac{2}{5}$

a) $\frac{3}{4}$ b) $\frac{6}{50}$

c) $\frac{6}{15}$ d) $\frac{4}{3}$ (1 mark)

Score   / 5

Answer all parts of the questions.

1 Fill in the blanks in these equivalent fractions.

a) $\frac{2}{11} = \frac{4}{\Box}$ b) $\frac{4}{7} = \frac{\Box}{49}$ c) $\frac{25}{100} = \frac{1}{\Box}$ d) $\frac{12}{17} = \frac{36}{\Box}$ (4 marks)

2 Change these improper fractions to mixed fractions.

a) $\frac{5}{2} =$ ....   b) $\frac{5}{3} =$ ....   c) $\frac{9}{2} =$ ....   d) $\frac{12}{11} =$ .... (4 marks)

3 Work out the answers to the following.

a) $\frac{2}{9} + \frac{1}{3}$ ....   b) $\frac{7}{11} - \frac{1}{4}$ ....   c) $\frac{4}{7} \times \frac{3}{8}$ ....   d) $\frac{9}{12} \div \frac{1}{4}$ ....

e) $\frac{5}{7} - \frac{1}{21}$ ....   f) $\frac{4}{9} + \frac{3}{27}$ ....   g) $\frac{7}{12} \times 1\frac{1}{2}$ ....   h) $1\frac{4}{7} \div \frac{7}{12}$ .... (8 marks)

4 Arrange these fractions in order of size, smallest first.

a) $\frac{2}{3}$ $\frac{4}{5}$ $\frac{1}{7}$ $\frac{3}{4}$ $\frac{1}{2}$ $\frac{3}{10}$ b) $\frac{5}{8}$ $\frac{1}{3}$ $\frac{2}{7}$ $\frac{1}{4}$ $\frac{3}{4}$ $\frac{2}{5}$

.... (2 marks)   .... (2 marks)

5 Decide whether these statements are true or false.

a) $\frac{4}{5}$ of 20 is bigger than $\frac{6}{7}$ of 14 .... (1 mark)

b) $\frac{2}{9}$ of 27 is smaller than $\frac{1}{3}$ of 15 .... (1 mark)

Score   / 22

c **These are GCSE style questions. Answer all parts of the questions. Show your workings (on separate paper if necessary) and include the correct units in your answers.**

1 Gill says 'I've got three fifths of a bottle of orange juice.'

Jonathan says 'I've got two thirds of a bottle of orange juice and my bottle of orange juice is the same size as yours.'

Who has got the most orange juice, Gill or Jonathan? Explain your answer.

....

.... (2 marks)

2 Work out these.

a) $\frac{2}{3} + \frac{4}{5}$ .... (1 mark)

b) $\frac{9}{11} - \frac{1}{3}$ .... (1 mark)

c) $\frac{2}{7} \times \frac{4}{9}$ .... (1 mark)

d) $\frac{3}{10} \div \frac{2}{5}$ .... (1 mark)

3 Charlotte's take home pay is £930. She gives her mother $\frac{1}{3}$ of this and spends $\frac{1}{5}$ of the £930 on going out. What fraction of the £930 is left? Give your answer as a fraction in its lowest terms.

....

.... (3 marks)

4 In a class of 32 pupils, $\frac{1}{8}$ are left-handed. How many students are not left-handed?

.... (1 mark)

Score   / 10

How well did you do?

1–11 marks   Try again
12–20 marks   Getting there
21–30 marks   Good work
31–37 marks   Excellent!

TOTAL SCORE   / 37

For more information on this topic see pages 8–9 of your Success Guide.

DECIMALS

NUMBER

A Choose just one answer, a, b, c or d.

1 Here are some discs.

5.8 5.79 5.81 5.805

Which of these discs has the largest number?
a) 5.8   b) 5.79
c) 5.81   d) 5.805   (1 mark)

2 Work out the answer to 9.45 × 5
a) 47.52   b) 56.7
c) 47.25   d) 46.75   (1 mark)

3 If a piece of cheese weighs 0.3 kg, how much would 70 identical pieces of cheese weigh?
a) 2.1 kg   b) 21 kg
c) 0.21 kg d) 210 kg   (1 mark)

4 Work out the answer to 520 ÷ 0.02
a) 2600   b) 260
c) 260 000 d) 26 000   (1 mark)

5 Round 18.629 to 2 decimal places
a) 18.69   b) 18.63
c) 18.7   d) 18.62   (1 mark)

Score   / 5

B Answer all parts of the questions.

1 Look at these statements and decide whether they are true or false.

a) 0.72 is bigger than 0.724 .... (1 mark)

b) 6.427 rounded to 2 decimal places is 6.43 .... (1 mark)

c) 12.204 is smaller than 12.214 .... (1 mark)

d) 37.465 rounded to 1 decimal place is 37.5 .... (1 mark)

e) 27.406 rounded to 2 decimal places is 27.41 .... (1 mark)

2 Here are some number cards. 7.32 7.09 8.31 8.315 7.102 7.321

Arrange these number cards in order of size, smallest first. ☐☐☐☐☐☐ (2 marks)

3 Four friends run a race. Their times in seconds are shown in the table below.

Thomas	Hussain	Molly	Joshua
14.072	15.12	14.07	16.321

a) Who won the race? .... (1 mark)

b) What is the difference between Hussain and Joshua's time? .... (1 mark)

c) How much faster was Molly than Thomas? .... (1 mark)

4 Here are some calculations. Fill in the gaps to make the statements correct.

a) 640 ÷ 40 = ...   b) 500 × 0.2 = ...   c) 600 ÷ 0.3 ....

d) 40 ÷ .... = 400   e) .... × 0.02 = 0.48   f) 420 ÷ .... = 42 000   (6 marks)

Score   / 16

12

C

These are GCSE style questions. Answer all parts of the questions. Show your workings (on separate paper if necessary) and include the correct units in your answers.

1 Here are some number cards.

| 6.14 | 7.29 | 7.42 | 7.208 | 6.141 |

a) Arrange these cards in order of size, smallest first.

(2 marks)

b) Work out the difference between the highest number and the smallest number.

.... (1 mark)

c) What is the total of all of these cards?

.... (1 mark)

d) To play a game, the cards need to be rounded to 2 decimal places.

Round the cards below to 2 decimal places.

| 7.208 | 6.141 |

i) 7.208 becomes   .... (1 mark)

ii) 6.141 becomes   .... (1 mark)

2 Here are some number cards.

| 0.1 | 0.01 | 0.001 | 100 | 10 |

Use one of the number cards to fill the gaps to make the statements correct.

a) 60 ÷ .... = 6 000 (1 mark)

b) 25 × .... = 2.5 (1 mark)

c) 720 ÷ .... = 720 000 (1 mark)

Score   / 9

How well did you do?

1–7 marks   Try again
8–15 marks   Getting there
16–23 marks   Good work
24–30 marks   Excellent!

TOTAL SCORE   / 30

For more information on this topic see pages 10–11 of your Success Guide.

PERCENTAGES 1

Choose just one answer, a, b, c or d.

1 Work out 10% of £850.
a) £8.50
b) £0.85
c) £85
d) £42.50   (1 mark)

2 Work out $17\frac{1}{2}$% of £60.
a) £9
b) £15
c) £10.50
d) £12.50   (1 mark)

3 In a survey, 17 people out of 25 said they preferred type A cola. What percentage of people preferred type A cola?
a) 68%   b) 60%
c) 72%   d) 75%   (1 mark)

4 A CD player costs £60 in a sale after a reduction of 20%. What was the original price of the CD player?
a) £48
b) £70
c) £72
d) £75   (1 mark)

5 A new car was bought for £15 000. Two years later it was sold for £12 000. What is the percentage loss?
a) 25%
b) 20%
c) 80%
d) 70%   (1 mark)

Score   / 5

Answer all parts of the questions.

1 Match the calculations with the correct answer. The first has been done for you.

10% of 30	16
40% of 40	5
5% of 15	3
25% of 20	0.75

(3 marks)

2 Colin earns £25 500 a year. This year he has a 3% pay rise. How much per year does Colin now earn?

£ ....   (2 marks)

3 A coat costs £140. In a sale it is reduced to £85. What is the percentage reduction?

.... %   (2 marks)

4 Lucinda scored 58 out of 75 in a test. What percentage did she get?

.... %   (2 marks)

5 The cost for a ticket for a concert has risen by 15% to £23. What was the ticket's original price?

£ ....   (2 marks)

6 12 out of 30 people wear glasses. What percentage wear glasses?

.... %   (2 marks)

Score   / 13

C These are GCSE style questions. Answer all parts of the questions. Show your workings (on separate paper if necessary) and include the correct units in your answers.

1 The price of a television set is £175 plus VAT. VAT is charged at a rate of 17.5%.

a) Work out the amount of VAT charged.

.... (2 marks)

b) In a sale, normal prices are reduced by 15%.
The normal price of a washing machine is £399.

Work out the sale price of the washing machine.

.... (3 marks)

2 A car is bought for £17 900. Two years later it is sold for £14 320.
Work out the percentage   loss.

.... %   (3 marks)

3 In a sale, all normal prices are reduced by 18%. In the sale Suki pays £57.40 for a jacket.

Calculate the normal price of the jacket.

.... (3 marks)

Score   / 11

How well did you do?
1–7 marks   Try again
8–16 marks   Getting there
17–23 marks   Good work
24–29 marks   Excellent!

TOTAL SCORE   / 29

For more information on this topic see pages 12–13 of your Success Guide.

PERCENTAGES 2

Choose just one answer, a, b, c or d.

1 £2 000 is invested in a savings account. Compound interest is paid at 2.1%. How much interest is paid after 2 years?
a) £4
b) £5.20
c) £2.44
d) £84.88   (1 mark)

2 A bike was bought for £120. Each year it depreciated by 10%. What was the bike worth 2 years later?
a) £97.20
b) £98
c) £216
d) £110   (1 mark)

3 Roberto has £5 000 in his savings account. Simple interest is paid at 3%. How much does he have in his savings account at the end of the year?
a) £4 850
b) £5 010
c) £5 150
d) £5 140.50   (1 mark)

4 Lucy earns £23 500. National Insurance (NI) is deducted at 9%. How much NI must she pay?
a) £2 250
b) £2 115
c) £2 200
d) £21 385   (1 mark)

Score   / 4

Answer all parts of the questions.

1 A meal costs £143. VAT at 17½% is added to the price of the meal. What is the final price of the meal?

£ ....
(2 marks)

2 VAT of 5% is added to a gas bill of £72. Find the total amount to be paid.

£ ....
(2 marks)

3 A motorbike is bought for £9 000. Each year it depreciates in value by 12%. Work out the value of the motorbike after 2 years.

£ ....
(2 marks)

4 Caroline has £6 200 in her savings account. If compound interest is paid at 2.7% p.a., how much interest will she earn after 3 years?

£ ....
(2 marks)

5 A house was bought for £112 000. After the first year the price had increased by 8%, during the second year it increased in price by a further 12%. What is the house now worth?

£ ....
(2 marks)

6 Petrol cost 74.9 pence per litre. The price increased by 2%. Six months later it increased again, by 5%. How much does a litre of petrol now cost?

.... pence
(2 marks)

Score   / 12

C These are GCSE style questions. Answer all parts of the questions. Show your workings (on separate paper if necessary) and include the correct units in your answers.

1 a) Work out 40% of £2 500.

.... (2 marks)

b) Find the simple interest on £2 000 invested for 2 years at 4% per year.

.... (3 marks)

2 £7 000 is invested for 3 years at 6% compound interest.

Work out the total interest earned over the three years.

.... (3 marks)

3 Nigel opened an account with £450 at his local bank. After one year, the bank paid him interest. He then had £465.75 in his account.

a) Work out, as a percentage, his local bank's interest rate.

....

....

.... (3 marks)

b) Lucy opened an account at the same bank as Nigel. She invested £700 for 2 years at 4% compound interest. How much money did she have in her account after 2 years?

....

....

.... (3 marks)

Score   / 14

How well did you do?

1–7 marks	Try again
8–12 marks	Getting there
13–21 marks	Good work
22–30 marks	Excellent!

TOTAL SCORE   / 30

For more information on this topic see pages 14–15 of your Success Guide.

FRACTIONS, DECIMALS AND PERCENTAGES

A Choose just one answer, a, b, c or d.

1 What is $\frac{3}{5}$ as a percentage?
a) 30%
b) 25%
c) 60%
d) 75%   (1 mark)

2 What is $\frac{2}{3}$ written as a decimal?
a) 0.77
b) 0.6̇6̇
c) 0.665
d) 0.6   (1 mark)

3 What is the smallest value in this list of numbers: 29%, 0.4, $\frac{3}{4}$, $\frac{1}{8}$?
a) 29%
b) 0.4
c) $\frac{3}{4}$
d) $\frac{1}{8}$ (1 mark)

4 What is the largest value from this list of numbers: $\frac{4}{5}$, 80%, $\frac{2}{3}$, 0.9?
a) $\frac{4}{5}$
b) 80%
c) $\frac{2}{3}$
d) 0.9   (1 mark)

5 Change $\frac{5}{8}$ into a decimal.
a) 0.625
b) 0.425
c) 0.125
d) 0.725   (1 mark)

Score   / 5

B Answer all parts of the questions.

1 The table shows equivalent fractions, decimals and percentages. Fill in the gaps.

Fraction	Decimal	Percentage
$\frac{2}{5}$		
		5%
	0.3̇	
	0.04	
		25%
$\frac{1}{8}$		

(6 marks)

2 Put these cards in order of size, smallest first.

| 0.31 | 30% | $\frac{3}{8}$ | $\frac{1}{3}$ | 92% | $\frac{1}{2}$ | 0.62 |

⬚ ⬚ ⬚ ⬚ ⬚ ⬚ ⬚   (2 marks)

3 A sundial is being sold in two different garden centres. The cost of the sundial is £89.99 in both garden centres. Both garden centres have a promotion.

Gardens are Us

Sundial 22% off

Rosebushes

Sundial $\frac{1}{4}$ off

In which garden centre is the sundial the cheapest? Explain your reasoning.

....

.... (2 marks)

Score   / 10

18

C These are GCSE style questions. Answer all parts of the questions. Show your workings (on separate paper if necessary) and include the correct units in your answers.

1 Write this list of seven numbers in order of size. Start with the smallest number.

25% $\frac{1}{3}$ 0.27 $\frac{2}{5}$ 0.571   72% $\frac{7}{8}$

.... (3 marks)

2 Philippa is buying a new television. She sees three different advertisements for the same television set.

Ed's Electricals

TV normal price

£250

Sale 10% off

Sheila's Bargains

TV **£185** plus

VAT at $17\frac{1}{2}$%

GITA's TV SHOP

Normal price

£290

Sale: $\frac{1}{5}$ off normal price

a) Find the maximum and minimum prices that Philippa could pay for a television set.

Maximum price = ...

Minimum price = ... (7 marks)

b) The price of the television in a fourth shop is £235. This includes VAT at $17\frac{1}{2}$%. Work out the cost of the television before VAT is added.

.... (3 marks)

3 Decide whether these calculations give the same answer for this question:

Increase £40 by 20%

Jack says: Multiply 40 by 1.2

Hannah says: Work out 10%, double it and then add on to 40

.... (2 marks)

Score   / 15

How well did you do?

1–7 marks	Try again
8–13 marks	Getting there
14–22 marks	Good work
23–30 marks	Excellent!

TOTAL SCORE   **/ 30**

For more information on this topic see page 16 of your Success Guide.

APPROXIMATIONS AND USING A CALCULATOR

A Choose just one answer, a, b, c or d.

1 Estimate the answer to the calculation 27×41.
a) 1 107
b) 1 200
c) 820
d) 1 300 (1 mark)

2 A carton of orange juice costs 79p. Estimate the cost of 402 cartons of orange juice.
a) £350
b) £250
c) £400
d) £320 (1 mark)

3 A school trip is organised. 407 pupils are going on the trip. Each coach seats 50 pupils. Approximately how many coaches are needed?
a) 12   b) 5
c) 8   d) 10 (1 mark)

4 Estimate the answer to the calculation $\frac{(4.2)^2}{107}$
a) 16
b) 1.6
c) 0.16
d) 160 (1 mark)

5 Round 5379 to three significant figures.
a) 538
b) 5 370
c) 537
d) 5 380 (1 mark)

Score   / 5

B Answer all parts of the questions.

1 Decide whether each statement is true or false.

a) 2.742 rounded to 3 significant figures is 2.74 ....

b) 2793 rounded to 2 significant figures is 27 ....

c) 32 046 rounded to 1 significant figure is 40 000 ....

d) 14.637 rounded to 3 significant figures is 14.6 .... (4 marks)

2 Round each of the numbers in the calculations to 1 significant figure and work out an approximate answer.

a) $\frac{(32.9)^2}{9.1}$ ....

b) $\frac{(906 \div 31.4)^2}{7.1 + 2.9}$ .... (2 marks)

3 Work these out on your calculator. Give your answers to 3 s.f.

a) $\frac{4.2(3.6 + 5.1)}{2 - 1.9}$ ....

b) $\frac{6 \times \sqrt{12.1}}{4.2}$ ....

c) $\frac{12^5}{4.3 \times 9.15}$ ....

(3 marks)

Score   / 9

C These are GCSE style questions. Answer all parts of the questions. Show your workings (on separate paper if necessary) and include the correct units in your answers.

1 a) Write down two numbers you could use to get an approximate answer to this question.

31 × 79 .... and .... (1 mark)

b) Work out your approximate answer.

.... (1 mark)

c) Work out the difference between your approximate answer and the exact answer.

.... (2 marks)

2 Use your calculator to work out the value of the sum below. Give your answer correct to 3 significant figures.

$$\frac{\sqrt{4.9^2 + 6.3}}{2.1 \times 0.37}$$

.... (3 marks)

3 a) Use your calculator to work out the value of this. Write down all the figures on your calculator display.

$$\frac{27.1 \times 6.2}{38.2 - 9.9}$$

.... (2 marks)

b) Round each of the numbers in the above calculation to 1 significant figure and obtain an approximate answer.

.... (3 marks)

4 Estimate the answer to the following. Leave your answer as a fraction in its simplest form.

$$\frac{21.2^2 - 10.3^2}{3.6 \times 29}$$

.... (3 marks)

5 a) Use your calculator to work out the value of the following. Write down all the figures on your calculator display.

$$\frac{(15.2 + 6.9)^2}{3.63 - 4.2}$$

.... (2 marks)

b) Round your answer to 3 significant figures. .... (1 mark)

Score   / 18

How well did you do?

1–10 marks   Try again
11–16 marks   Getting there
17–22 marks   Good work
23–32 marks   Excellent!

TOTAL SCORE   / 29

For more information on this topic see pages 17–19 of your Success Guide.

RATIO

A **Choose just one answer, a, b, c or d.**

1 What is the ratio 6 : 18 written in its simplest form?
a) 3 : 1
b) 3 : 9
c) 1 : 3
d) 9 : 3 (1 mark)

2 Write the ratio 200 : 500 in the form 1 : n.
a) 1 : 50
b) 1 : 5
c) 1 : 25
d) 1 : 2.5 (1 mark)

3 If £140 is divided in the ratio 3 : 4, what is the size of the larger share?
a) £45 b) £60
c) £80 d) £90 (1 mark)

4 A recipe for 4 people needs 800 g of flour. How much flour is needed for 6 people?
a) 12 g
b) 120 g
c) 12 kg
d) 1200 g (1 mark)

5 If 9 oranges cost £1.08, how much would 14 similar oranges cost?
a) £1.50
b) £1.68
c) £1.20
d) £1.84 (1 mark)

Score /5

B **Answer all parts of the questions.**

1 Write down each of the following ratios in the form 1 : n.

a) 10 : 15 .... (1 mark)

b) 6 : 10 .... (1 mark)

c) 9 : 27 .... (1 mark)

2 Seven bottles of lemonade have a total capacity of 1680 ml. Work out the total capacity for five similar bottles.

.... (1 mark)

3 a) Increase £4.10 in the ratio 2 : 5. .... (1 mark)

b) Decrease 120 g in the ratio 5 : 2. .... (1 mark)

4 Mrs London inherited £55 000. She divided the money between her children in the ratio 3 : 3 : 5. How much did the child with the largest share receive?

£ .... (2 marks)

5 It takes 6 men 3 days to dig and lay a cable. How long would it take 4 men?

.... days (2 marks)

Score / 10

C   These are GCSE style questions. Answer all parts of the questions. Show your workings (on separate paper if necessary) and include the correct units in your answers.

1   Vicky and Tracy share £14 400 in the ratio 4 : 5. Work out how much each of them receives.

Vicky £............................   Tracy £............................   (3 marks)

2   James uses these ingredients to make 12 buns.

50 g butter
40 g sugar
2 eggs
45 g flour
15 ml milk

James wants to make 30 similar buns. Write down how much of each ingredient he needs for 30 buns.

butter .... g   sugar .... g

eggs ....   flour .... g

milk ....   (3 marks)

3   It takes 3 builders 16 days to build a wall. All the builders work at the same rate.

How long would it take 8 builders to build a wall the same size?

.... (3 marks)

Score   / 9

How well did you do?

1–6 marks	Try again
7–11 marks	Getting there
12–18 marks	Good work
19–24 marks	Excellent!

TOTAL SCORE   / 24

For more information on this topic see pages 20–21 of your Success Guide.

INDICES

Choose just one answer, a, b, c or d.

1 In index form, what is the value of $8^3 \times 8^{11}$?
   a) 8^{14}
   b) 8^{33}
   c) 64^{14}
   d) 64^{33} (1 mark)

2 In index form, what is the value of $(4^2)^3$?
   a) 12^2
   b) 4^5
   c) 4^6
   d) 16^6 (1 mark)

3 What is the value of 5^0?
   a) 5
   b) 0
   c) 25
   d) 1 (1 mark)

4 What is the value of 5^{-2}?
   a) $\frac{1}{25}$
   b) -5
   c) 25
   d) -25 (1 mark)

5 What is the value of $7^{-12} \div 7^2$ written in index form?
   a) 7^{10}
   b) 7^{-14}
   c) 7^{14}
   d) 7^{-10} (1 mark)

Score   / 5

Answer all parts of the questions.

1 Work out the exact value of these.

   a) 4^3 ....   b) 2^5 ....   c) 3^4 .... (3 marks)

2 Decide whether each of these expressions is true or false.

   a) $a^4 \times a^5 = a^{20}$ ....

   b) $2a^4 \times 3a^2 = 5a^8$ ....

   c) $10a^6 \div 2a^4 = 5a^2$ ....

   d) $20a^4b^2 \div 10a^5b = 2a^{-1}b$ ....

   e) $(2a^3)^3 = 6a^9$ ....

   f) $4^0 = 1$ .... (6 marks)

3 Simplify the following expressions.

   a) $3a \times 2a =$ ....

   b) $12m^3 \div 4m =$ ....

   c) $10a^2b^4 \times 2ab =$ ....

   d) $(5a)^0 =$ ....

   e) $(2a^2)^4 =$ ....

   f) $12a^4 \div 16a^7 =$ ....

   g) $(a^4)^5 =$ ....

   h) $(3a^2b^3)^3 =$ .... (8 marks)

4 Find the value of n in each of the following.

   a) $8^{10} \times 8^n = 8^{16}$ ....

   b) $10^n \div 10^{-2} = 10^{12}$ ....

   c) $(4^n)^3 = 4^{27}$ .... (3 marks)

5 Write these using negative indices.

   a) $\frac{4}{x^2} =$ ....

   b) $\frac{a^2}{b^3} =$ ....

   c) $\frac{3}{y^5} =$ .... (3 marks)

Score   / 23

C These are GCSE style questions. Answer all parts of the questions. Show your workings (on separate paper if necessary) and include the correct units in your answers.

1 Simplify these.

a) $p^3 \times p^4$ ....

b) $\dfrac{n^3}{n^7}$ ....

c) $\dfrac{a^3 \times a^4}{a}$ ....

d) $\dfrac{12a^2b}{3a}$ ....

(4 marks)

2 Work out these.

a) 3^0 ....

b) 5^{-2} ....

c) $3^4 \times 2^3$ ....

(3 marks)

3 a) Evaluate the following.

i) 8^0 ....

ii) 4^{-2} ....

iii) $16^{\frac{1}{2}}$ ....

(3 marks)

b) Write this as a single power of 5.

$\dfrac{5^7 \times 5^3}{(5^2)^3}$ ....

(2 marks)

4 Simplify these.

a) $2a^3 \times 3a^2$ ....

b) $\dfrac{12a^2b}{4ab}$ ....

c) $\dfrac{b^6 \times 3b^2}{12b^{10}}$ ....

(3 marks)

5 Evaluate the following.

a) i) 4^0 .... ii) $25^{\frac{1}{2}}$ .... iii) 2^{-3} .... (3 marks)

b) Write $\dfrac{3^4 \times 3^6}{3^{20}}$ as a single power of 3.

.... (2 marks)

Score   / 20

How well did you do?

1–11 marks   Try again
12–24 marks   Getting there
25–30 marks   Good work
36–48 marks   Excellent!

TOTAL SCORE   / 48

For more information on this topic see pages 22–23 of your Success Guide.

STANDARD INDEX FORM

A

Choose just one answer, a, b, c or d.

1 What is this number written in standard form?   **42 710**
a) 42.71×10^3
b) 4.271×10^4
c) 4271.0×10
d) 427.1×10^2 (1 mark)

2 What is 6.4×10^{-3} written as an ordinary number?
a) 6 400
b) 0.006 4
c) 64
d) 0.064   (1 mark)

3 What is 2.7×10^4 written as an ordinary number?
a) 27 000   b) 0.27
c) 270   d) 0.000 27   (1 mark)

4 What would $(4 \times 10^9) \times (2 \times 10^6)$ worked out and written in standard form be?
a) 8×10^{54}
b) 8×10^{15}
c) 8×10^3
d) 6×10^{15} (1 mark)

5 What would $(3 \times 10^4)^2$ worked out and written in standard form be?
a) 9×10^6
b) 9×10^8
c) 9×10^9
d) 3×10^8 (1 mark)

Score   / 5

B

Answer all parts of the questions.

1 Write these numbers in standard form.

a) 2710 = ...

b) 4 270 000 ....

c) 0.0271 = ...

d) 0.0036 ....

e) 4 million = ...

f) 0.000 41 .... (6 marks)

2 Decide whether each of the statements is true or false.

a) 4710 is 4.71×10^3 written in standard form. ....

b) 249 000 is 24.9×10^4 written in standard form. ....

c) 0.047 is 47×10^{-3} written in standard form. ....

d) 0.000 009 6 is 9.6×10^{-7} written in standard form. .... (4 marks)

3 Carry out the following calculations. Give your answer in standard form.

a) $(4 \times 10^6) \times (2 \times 10)$ ....

b) $(7 \times 10^{-3}) \times (2 \times 10^6)$ ....

c) $(9 \times 10^{12}) \div (3 \times 10^{-4})$ ....

d) $(2.4 \times 10^{10}) \div (3 \times 10^6)$ .... (4 marks)

Score   / 14

C These are GCSE style questions. Answer all parts of the questions. Show your workings (on separate paper if necessary) and include the correct units in your answers.

1 a) i) Write the number 2.07×10^5 as an ordinary number.

....

ii) Write the number 0.000 046 in standard form.

.... (2 marks)

b) Multiply 7×10^4 by 5×10^7

Give your answer in standard form.

.... (2 marks)

2 Calculate the value of $\dfrac{4.68 \times 10^9 + 3.14 \times 10^7}{2.14 \times 10^{-3}}$

Give your answer in standard form, correct to 2 significant figures.

.... (3 marks)

3 3.8×10^8 seeds weigh 1 kilogram.

Each seed weighs the same.

Calculate the weight in grams of one seed.

Give your answer in standard form, correct to 2 significant figures.

.... (2 marks)

4 Work out these calculations. Give your answer in standard form.

a) $(2.1 \times 10^7) \times (3.9 \times 10^{-4})$ ....

b) $(6.3 \times 10^{-4}) \times (1.2 \times 10^7)$ ....

c) $(1.2 \times 10^{-7}) \div (2 \times 10^{-4})$ ....

d) $(8.9 \times 10^6) \div (4 \times 10^{-2})$ .... (4 marks)

5 The mass of an atom is 2×10^{-23} grams.

What is the total mass of 9×10^{15} of these atoms? .... g (2 marks)

Score   / 15

How well did you do?

1–10 marks   Try again
11–18 marks   Getting there
19–27 marks   Good work
28–34 marks   Excellent!

TOTAL SCORE   / 34

For more information on this topic see pages 24–25 of your Success Guide.

ALGEBRA 1

Choose just one answer, a, b, c, or d.

1 There are *n* books in a pile. Each book is 5 cm thick. What is the formula for the total height *h* of the pile of books?

a) $5n$ b) $h = 5n$

c) $h = \dfrac{n}{5}$ d) $h = \dfrac{5}{n}$ (1 mark)

2 What is the expression $4a + 3b - a + 6b$ when it is fully simplified?

a) $9b - 3a$ b) $3a9b$

c) $3a + 9b$ d) $5a + 9b$ (1 mark)

3 What is the expression $7a - 4b + 6a - 3b$ when it is fully simplified?

a) $7b - a$ b) $13a + 7b$

c) $a - 7b$ d) $13a - 7b$ (1 mark)

4 If $a = \dfrac{b}{c}$ and $b = 12$ and $c = 4$, what is the value of *a*?

a) 12   b) 4

c) 6   d) 3   (1 mark)

5 If $m = \sqrt{\dfrac{r^2 p}{4}}$ and $r = 3$ and $p = 6$, what is the value of *m* to 1 decimal place?

a) 13.5   b) 182.3

c) 3.7   d) 3   (1 mark)

Score   / 5

Answer all parts of the questions.

1 Decide whether these expressions, which have been simplified, are true or false.

a) $3a - 2b + 5a + b = 8a - b$ .... (1 mark)

b) $6ay - 3ay^2 + 2ay^2 - 4ay = 2ay - ay^2$ .... (1 mark)

c) $3ab + 2a^2b - a^2b + 4ba = a^2b + 3ab + 4ba$ .... (1 mark)

2 John buys *b* books costing £6 each and *m* magazines costing 67 pence each. Write down a formula for the total cost (*T*) of the books and magazines.

$T =$ .... (2 marks)

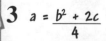**3** $a = \dfrac{b^2 + 2c}{4}$

a) Calculate *a* if $b = 2$ and $c = 6$. .... (1 mark)

b) Calculate *a* if $b = 3$ and $c = 5.5$. .... (1 mark)

c) Calculate *b* if $a = 25$ and $c = 18$. .... (1 mark)

Score   / 8

C These are GCSE style questions. Answer all parts of the questions. Show your workings (on separate paper if necessary) and include the correct units in your answers.

1 a) Simplify this fully.

$7n - 4n + 3n$ .... (1 mark)

b) Simplify this fully.

$3a \times 2b$ .... (1 mark)

2 a) Write in symbols the rule 'to find p, multiply n by 5 and then subtract 6'.

.... (1 mark)

b) Work out the value of p when $n = -2$.

.... (1 mark)

3 Peter uses this formula to calculate the value of V.

$$V = \frac{\pi x(2R^2 + t^2)}{500}$$

$\pi = 3.14, \quad x = 20, \quad R = 5.2, \quad t = -4.1$

Calculate the value of V, giving your answer to 2 significant figures.

$V =$ .... (3 marks)

4 Charlotte is given a formula in Physics: $v^2 - u^2 + 2as$

Charlotte works out the answer where $u = -5$, $a = 10$, $s = 0.6$.

She writes $v^2 = -5^2 + 2 \times 10 \times 0.6$
$v^2 = 25 + 12$
$v = 37$

Explain what Charlotte has done wrong. ....

.... (2 marks)

Score   / 9

How well did you do?

1–4 marks   Try again
5–9 marks   Getting there
10–16 marks   Good work
17–22 marks   Excellent!

TOTAL SCORE   / 22

For more information on this topic see pages 28–29 of your Success Guide.

ALGEBRA 2

A Choose just one answer, a, b, c or d.

1 What is the expression $3(2x - 1)$ when it is multiplied out and simplified?
- a) $6x - 3$
- b) $6x - 1$
- c) $2x - 3$
- d) $6x + 3$ (1 mark)

2 Factorise fully the expression $25x + 15$.
- a) $5(5x + 15)$
- b) $25(x + 15)$
- c) $5(5x + 3)$
- d) $5(5x)$ (1 mark)

3 What is $(n - 3)^2$ when it is multiplied out and simplified?
- a) $n^2 + 9$
- b) $n^2 + 6n - 9$
- c) $n^2 - 6n - 9$
- d) $n^2 - 6n + 9$ (1 mark)

4 $P = a^2 + b$. Rearrange this formula to make a the subject.
- a) $a = \pm\sqrt{P - b}$
- b) $a = \pm\sqrt{P + b}$
- c) $a = \dfrac{P - b}{2}$
- d) $a = \dfrac{P + b}{2}$ (1 mark)

5 Factorising $n^2 + 7n - 8$ gives:
- a) $(n - 2)(n - 6)$
- b) $(n - 2)(n + 4)$
- c) $(n - 1)(n + 8)$
- d) $(n + 1)(n - 8)$ (1 mark)

Score / 5

B Answer all parts of the questions.

1 Some expressions are written on card. Copy an expression in each space to make the statement correct.

| $3n - 3$ | $8(n + 2)$ | $n^2 - 3n + 2$ | $n^2 + 2$ | $5(n + 3)$ | $3n - 9$ |

a) $3(n - 3) = $ ....

b) $5n + 15 = $ ....

c) $(n - 1)(n - 2) = $ ....

d) $8n + 16 = $ ....

(4 marks)

2 Factorise the following expressions.

a) $10n + 15$ ....

b) $24 - 36n$ ....

c) $n^2 + 6n + 5$ ....

d) $n^2 - 64$ ....

e) $n^2 - 3n - 4$ ....

(5 marks)

3 Rearrange each of the formulas below to make b the subject.

a) $p = 3b - 4$ .... (1 mark)

b) $y = \dfrac{b^2 - 6}{4}$ .... (1 mark)

c) $5(n + b) = 2b + 2$ .... (1 mark)

Score / 12

C These are GCSE style questions. Answer all parts of the questions. Show your workings (on separate paper if necessary) and include the correct units in your answers.

1 **a)** Expand and simplify $3(2x + 1) - 2(x - 2)$

.... (2 marks)

    b) **i)** Factorise $6a + 12$ .... (1 mark)

        ii) Factorise completely $10a^2 - 15ab$ .... (2 marks)

    c) **i)** Factorise $n^2 + 5n + 6$ .... (2 marks)

        ii) Hence simplify fully $\dfrac{2(n + 3)}{n^2 + 5n + 6}$

        .... (2 marks)

    d) Factorise $(n + m)^2 - 2(n + m)$

    .... (2 marks)

2 In each of these questions, make x the subject of the formula.

    a) $p = \dfrac{x^2 + 3}{4}$

    .... (3 marks)

    b) $2(p + x) = 3x - 2$

    .... (3 marks)

3 Show that $(n - 1)^2 + n + (n - 1)$ simplifies to n^2.

....

....

....

.... (3 marks)

4 **a)** Expand and simplify $2(3a - 1) - (a - 2)$

    .... (2 marks)

    b) Factorise fully the following expressions.

        i) $3n - 12$ ....

        ii) $8p^2q - 12pq^2$ .... (2 marks)

    c) **i)** Factorise $a^2 + 4a - 5$ .... (2 marks)

        ii) Hence solve $a^2 + 4a - 5 = 0$

    .... (2 marks)

Score   / 30

How well did you do?

1–12 marks Try again
13–23 marks Getting there
24–34 marks Good work
35–45 marks Excellent!

TOTAL SCORE   / 47

For more information on this topic see pages 30–31 of your Success Guide.

EQUATIONS

A

Choose just one answer, a, b, c or d.

1 Solve the equation $4n - 2 = 10$
 a) $n = 4$
 b) $n = 2$
 c) $n = 3$
 d) $n = 3.5$ (1 mark)

2 Solve the equation $\frac{n}{2} + 4 = 2$
 a) $n = -4$
 b) $n = 4$
 c) $n = 12$
 d) $n = -12$ (1 mark)

3 Solve the equation $4(x + 3) = 16$
 a) $x = 9$
 b) $x = 7$
 c) $x = 4$
 d) $x = 1$ (1 mark)

4 Solve the equation $4(n + 2) = 8(n - 3)$
 a) $n = 16$
 b) $n = 8$
 c) $n = 4$
 d) $n = 12$ (1 mark)

5 Solve the equation $10 - 6n = 4n - 5$
 a) $n = 2$
 b) $n = -2$
 c) $n = 1.5$
 d) $n = -1.5$ (1 mark)

Score   / 5

B

Answer all parts of the questions.

1 Solve the following equations.

 a) $5n = 25$ ....
 b) $\frac{n}{3} = 12$ ....

 c) $2n - 4 = 10$ ....
 d) $3 - 2n = 14$ ....

 e) $\frac{n}{5} + 2 = 7$ ....
 f) $4 - \frac{n}{2} = 2$ .... (6 marks)

2 Solve the following equations.

 a) $12n + 5 = 3n + 32$ ....
 b) $5n - 4 = 3n + 6$ ....

 c) $5(n + 1) = 25$ ....
 d) $4(n - 2) = 3(n + 2)$ .... (4 marks)

3 Solve the following equations.

 a) $n^2 - 4n = 0$ ....
 b) $n^2 + 6n + 5 = 0$ ....

 c) $n^2 - 5n + 6 = 0$ ....
 d) $n^2 - 3n - 28 = 0$ .... (4 marks)

4 The angles in a triangle add up to 180°. Form an equation in n and solve it.

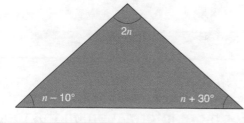
2n

n − 10°   n + 30°

$n =$ .... (2 marks)

Score   / 16

C These are GCSE style questions. Answer all parts of the questions. Show your workings (on separate paper if necessary) and include the correct units in your answers.

1 Solve these equations.

a) $5m - 3 = 12$

....

.... (2 marks)

b) $8p + 3 = 9 - 2p$

....

.... (2 marks)

c) $5(x - 1) = 3x + 7$

....

.... (2 marks)

d) $\dfrac{w}{2} + \dfrac{(3w + 2)}{3} = \dfrac{1}{3}$

....

.... (2 marks)

2 a) Factorise $x^2 - 4x + 3$ .... (2 marks)

b) Hence solve the equation $x^2 - 4x + 3 = 0$

$x =$ ....

and $x =$ .... (1 mark)

3 The lengths, in cm, of the sides of the triangle are $2x + 2$, $2x - 1$, $5x + 3$.

a) Write down, in terms of x, an expression for the perimeter of the triangle.

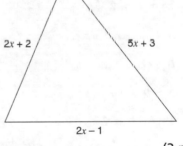

Give your expression in its simplest form.

.... (2 marks)

b) The perimeter of the triangle is 22 cm. Work out the length of the shortest side of the triangle.

....

.... (2 marks)

Score   / 17

TOTAL SCORE   / 38

For more information on this topic
see pages 32–33 of your Success Guide.

EQUATIONS AND INEQUALITIES

A

Choose just one answer, a, b, c or d.

1 Solve these simultaneous equations to find the values of a and b.

$a + b = 10 \quad 2a - b = 2$

a) $a = 4, b = 6$

b) $a = 4, b = -2$

c) $a = 5, b = 5$

d) $a = 3, b = 7$ (1 mark)

2 Solve these simultaneous equations to find the values of x and y.

$3x - y = 7 \quad 2x + y = 3$

a) $x = 3, y = 2$

b) $x = 2, y = 1$

c) $x = -3, y = 2$

d) $x = 2, y = -1$ (1 mark)

 3 The equation $y^3 + 2y = 82$ has a solution between 4 and 5. By using a method of trial and improvement, find the solution to 1 decimal place.

a) 3.9　　　　b) 4.1

c) 4.2　　　　d) 4.3 (1 mark)

4 Solve the inequality $3x + 1 < 19$

a) $x < 3$　　　　b) $x < 7$

c) $x < 5$　　　　d) $x < 6$ (1 mark)

5 Solve the inequality $2x - 7 < 9$

a) $x < 9$　　　　b) $x < 10$

c) $x < 8$　　　　d) $x < 6.5$ (1 mark)

Score / 5

B

Answer all parts of the questions.

1 Solve these simultaneous equations to find the values of a and b.

a) $2a + b = 8$

$3a - b = 2$

$a = \text{................................}$

$b = \text{................................}$ (2 marks)

b) $5a + b = 24$

$2a + 2b = 24$

$a = \text{................................}$

$b = \text{................................}$ (2 marks)

c) $a - b = 11$

$3a + 2b = 23$

$a = \text{................................}$

$b = \text{................................}$ (2 marks)

d) $4a + 3b = 6$

$2a - 3b = 12$

$a = \text{................................}$

$b = \text{................................}$ (2 marks)

2 Use a trial and improvement method to solve the following equation. Give your answer to 1 decimal place.

$t^2 - 2t = 20$ $t = \text{................................}$ (2 marks)

3 Solve the following inequalities.

a) $5x + 2 < 12$

$\text{................................}$ (1 mark)

b) $\frac{x}{3} + 1 \geq 3$

$\text{................................}$ (1 mark)

c) $3 \leq 2x + 1 \leq 9$

$\text{................................}$ (1 mark)

d) $3 \leq 3x + 2 \leq 8$

$\text{................................}$ (1 mark)

Score / 14

C These are GCSE style questions. Answer all parts of the questions. Show your workings (on separate paper if necessary) and include the correct units in your answers.

1 *n* is an integer.

a) Write down the values of *n* which satisfy the inequality $-4 < n \leq 2$

.... (2 marks)

b) Solve the inequality $5p - 2 \leq 8$ .... (2 marks)

2 Use the method of trial and improvement to solve the equation $x(3) + 3x = 28$

Give your answer correct to one decimal place.

You must show **all** your working

....

....

....

....

x = ... (4 marks)

3 Solve these simultaneous equations.

$3x - 2y = -12$

$2x + 6y = 3$

x = ...

y = ... (4 marks)

4 a) $2a - b = 0$ **b)** $5a + 4b = 23$

   $a + 3b = 7$ $3a - 5b = -1$

   a = ...   *a* = ...

   b = ...   *b* = ... (4 marks)

Score   / 16

How well did you do?

1–9 marks   Try again
10–19 marks Getting there
20–27 marks Good work
28–35 marks Excellent!

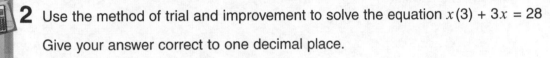

TOTAL SCORE   / 35

For more information on this topic
see pages 34–36 of your Success Guide.

NUMBER PATTERNS AND SEQUENCES

A Choose just one answer, a, b, c or d.

1 Here are the first four terms in a sequence:
1, 4, 9, 16
What is the next number in the sequence?
a) 24
b) 49
c) 36
d) 25 (1 mark)

2 What is the nth term of a sequence whose first four terms are 5, 7, 9, 11?
a) $2n + 3$
b) $2n - 3$
c) $n + 2$
d) $3 - 2n$ (1 mark)

3 If the nth term of a sequence is given by $4 - 3n$, what is the fifth term of this sequence?
a) −8
b) −2
c) −11
d) −14 (1 mark)

4 What is the nth term of a sequence whose first four terms are 18, 16, 14, 12?
a) $2n - 20$
b) $20 - 2n$
c) $n - 2$
d) $2n + 20$ (1 mark)

Score / 4

B Answer all parts of the questions.

1 Write down the next two terms in each of the sequences below.
a) 2, 4, 6, 8, ..., ...
b) 4, 7, 10, 13, ..., ...
c) 1, 4, 9, 16, ..., ...
d) 12, 6, 3, 1.5, ..., ... (4 marks)

2 The clouds below have some names of sequences.

Fibonacci   square numbers   triangular numbers   powers of 10   cube numbers

Match these sequences with the correct name.
a) 1, 1, 2, 3, 5, 8, 13 ....
b) 10, 100, 1000, 10 000 ....
c) 1, 8, 27, 64 .... (3 marks)

3 Look at this sequence: 7, 10, 13, 16.
a) What is the sixth number of this sequence? .... (1 mark)
b) Write down the nth term of this sequence. .... (1 mark)

4 Decide whether the nth term given is true or false for each of these sequences.
a) 1, 4, 7, 10, 13 nth term: $n + 3$ .... (1 mark)
b) 10, 6, 2, -2, -6 nth term: $10 - 4n$ .... (1 mark)
c) 1, 4, 7, 10 nth term: $3n - 2$ .... (1 mark)

Score / 12

C These are GCSE style questions. Answer all parts of the questions. Show your workings (on separate paper if necessary) and include the correct units in your answers.

1 a) Here are the first five terms of a sequence.

64, 32, 16, 8, 4

Write down the next three terms in the sequence.

.... , ... , ...　　　　(3 marks)

b) Here are the first five terms of a different sequence.

2, 7, 12, 17, 22

Find, in terms of n, an expression for the nth term of this sequence.

....　　　　(2 marks)

2 The nth term of the sequence given below is $2n + 1$.

3, 5, 7, 9 ...

Write down, in terms of n, the nth term for this sequence.

31, 51, 71, 91...

....　　　　(2 marks)

3 Here are the first four numbers in a sequence.

3, 7, 11, 15

Write down an expression for the nth term of this sequence.

....　　　　(2 marks)

4 Here are the first four terms of a sequence.

8, 6, 4, 2

Write down an expression for the nth term of the sequence.

....　　　　(2 marks)

Score　　/ 11

How well did you do?

1–5 marks　Try again
6–10 marks　Getting there
11–19 marks　Good work
20–27 marks　Excellent!

TOTAL SCORE　　/ 27

For more information on this topic see page 37 of your Success Guide.

STRAIGHT LINE GRAPHS

A

Choose just one answer, a, b, c or d.

1 Which pair of coordinates lie on the line $x = 2$?
   a) $(1, 3)$
   b) $(2, 3)$
   c) $(3, 2)$
   d) $(0, 2)$ (1 mark)

2 Which pair of coordinates lie on the line
   $y = -3$?
   a) $(-3, 5)$
   b) $(5, -2)$
   c) $(-2, 5)$
   d) $(5, -3)$ (1 mark)

3 What is the gradient of the line $y = 2 - 5x$?
   a) -2
   b) -5
   c) 2
   d) 5 (1 mark)

4 These graphs have been drawn:
   $y = 3x - 1, y = 5 - 2x,$
   $y = 6x + 1, y = 2x - 3$
   Which graph is the steepest?
   a) $y = 3x - 1$
   b) $y = 5 - 2x$
   c) $y = 6x + 1$
   d) $y = 2x - 3$ (1 mark)

5 At what point does the graph $y = 3x - 4$
   intercept the y axis?
   a) $(0, -4)$
   b) $(0, 3)$
   c) $(-4, 0)$
   d) $(3, 0)$ (1 mark)

Score   / 5

B

Answer all parts of the questions.

1 a) Complete the table of values for $y = 6 - x$.

x	-2	-1	0	1	2
$y = 6 - x$			6		4

(2 marks)

On the grid below, plot your values for x and y. Join your points with a straight line. (1 mark)

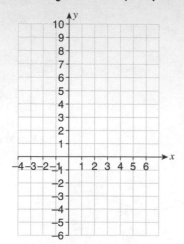

b) A second line goes through the coordinates
   (1, 5), (-2, -4) and (2, 8)

   i) Draw this line. (1 mark)

   ii) Write down the equation of the line you have just drawn.

   .... (2 marks)

c) What are the coordinates of the point where the two lines meet?

   .... (1 mark)

2 The equations of five straight lines are: $y = 2x - 4$, $y = 3 - 2x$, $y = 4 - 2x$, $y = 5x - 4$, $y = 3x - 5$

Two of the lines are parallel. Write down the equations of these two lines.

.... and .... (2 marks)

Score   / 9

C This is a GCSE style question. Answer all parts of the question. Show your workings (on separate paper if necessary) and include the correct units in your answers.

1 The line with equation $3y + 2x = 12$ has been drawn on the grid.

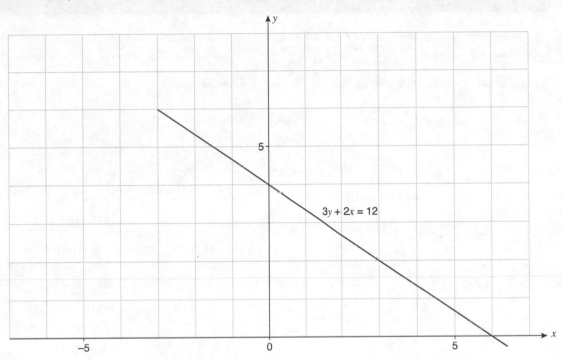

3y + 2x = 12

a) Write down the gradient of the line $3y + 2x = 12$

.... (2 marks)

b) Write down the equation of the line which is parallel to $3y + 2x = 12$ and passes through the point with coordinates (0, 2).

.... (1 mark)

c) On the grid above draw the graph with the equation $3y - x = 3$ (2 marks)

d) Write down the coordinates of the point of intersection of the two straight-line graphs.

(.............................. , ...) (1 mark)

Score /6

How well did you do?

1–4 marks Try again
5–9 marks Getting there
10–14 marks Good work
15–20 marks Excellent!

TOTAL SCORE /20

For more information on this topic see pages 38–39 of your Success Guide.

CURVED GRAPHS

A

Choose just one answer, a, b, c or d.

1 Which pair of coordinates lies on the graph $y = x^2 - 2$?
   a) $(1, 1)$
   b) $(4, 14)$
   c) $(2, 4)$
   d) $(0, 2)$ (1 mark)

2 On which of these curves do the coordinates $(2, 5)$ lie?
   a) $y = x^2 - 4$
   b) $y = 2x^2 + 3$
   c) $y = x^2 - 6$
   d) $y = 2x^2 - 3$ (1 mark)

Questions 3–5 refer to these diagrams.

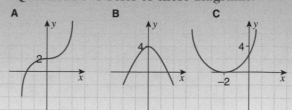

3 What is the equation of curve A?
   a) $y = 5 - 2x^2$ b) $y = x^2 + 4x + 4$
   c) $y = x^3 + 2$ d) $y = 4 - x^2$ (1 mark)

4 What is the equation of curve B?
   a) $y = 5 - 2x^2$ b) $y = x^2 + 4x + 4$
   c) $y = x^3 + 2$ d) $y = 4 - x^2$ (1 mark)

5 What is the equation of curve C?
   a) $y = 5 - 2x^2$ b) $y = x^2 + 4x + 4$
   c) $y = x^3 + 2$ d) $y = 4 - x^2$ (1 mark)

Score   / 5

B

Answer all parts of the questions.

1 a) Complete the table of values for $y = x^2 - 2x - 2$.

x	-2	-1	0	1	2	3
$y = x^2 - 2x - 2$			-2		1	

(2 marks)

   b) On the grid below draw the graph of $y = x^2 - 2x - 2$ (3 marks)

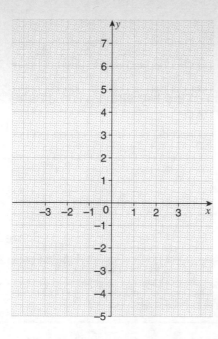

   c) Use your graph to write down an estimate for these.

   i) The minimum value of y

   $y =$ ....   (1 mark)

   ii) The solutions of the equation $x^2 - 2x - 2 = 0$

   $x =$ .... and $x =$ ....   (2 marks)

Score   / 8

C These are GCSE style questions. Answer all parts of the questions. Show your workings (on separate paper if necessary) and include the correct units in your answers.

1 **a)** Complete the table of values for the graph of $y = x^3 - 4$

x	−2	−1	0	1	2	3
$y = x^3 - 4$		−5				23

(2 marks)

b) On the grid, draw the graph of $y = x^3 - 4$

(2 marks)

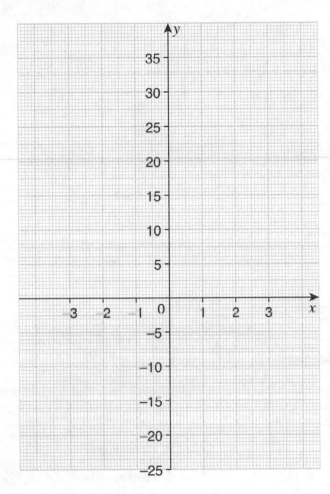

c) Use your graph to find an estimate of:

i) the solution of the equation $x^3 - 4 = 0$.

$x =$ .... (1 mark)

ii) the solution of the equation $x^3 - 4 = 10$

$x =$ .... (2 marks)

Score / 7

How well did you do?

1–4 marks Try again
5–9 marks Getting there
10–14 marks Good work
15–20 marks Excellent!

TOTAL SCORE   / 20

For more information on this topic see pages 40–41 of your Success Guide.

INTERPRETING GRAPHS

A

Choose just one answer, a, b, c or d.

1 If £1 = $1.48, how much would £10 be in American dollars?
a) $0.148   b) $148
c) $14.8   d) $1480   (1 mark)

For the next three questions use the graph opposite. The graph shows Mrs Morgan's car journey.

2 At what speed did Mrs Morgan travel for the first hour and a half?
a) 25 mph   b) 28 mph
c) 30 mph   d) 26.7 mph   (1 mark)

3 At what time did Mrs Morgan take a break from her car journey?
a) 1530   b) 1600
c) 1400   d) 1500   (1 mark)

4 At what speed did Mrs Morgan travel between 1700 and 1800 hours?
a) 60 mph   b) 80 mph
c) 35 mph   d) 40 mph   (1 mark)

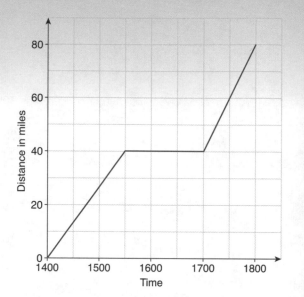

Score   / 4

B

Answer all parts of the questions.

1 Water is poured into these odd-shaped vases at a constant rate. Match each vase to the correct graph.

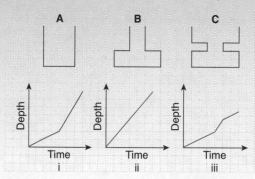

Vase A matches graph ....

Vase B matches graph ....

Vase C matches graph ....   (3 marks)

2 Match these graphs to the statements.

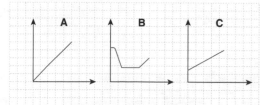

1 A mobile phone company charges a standard fee plus a certain amount per call.   Graph ....

2 The price of shares dropped sharply, levelled off and then started rising.   Graph ....

3 Conversion between kilometres and miles. Graph ....

(3 marks)

Score   / 6

C

This is a GCSE style question. Answer all parts of the question. Show your workings (on separate paper if necessary) and include the correct units in your answers.

1 William went for a cycle ride to the local market.

The distance–time graph shows his ride.

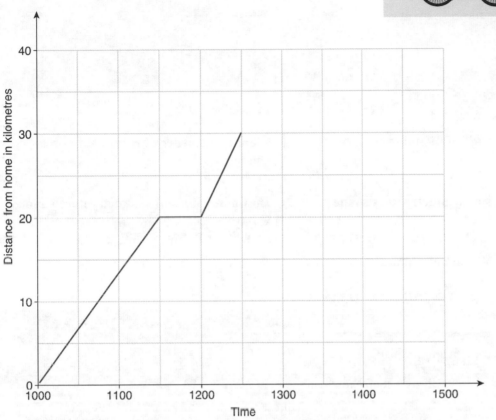

He set off from home at 1000, and arrived at the market at 1230.

a) Explain what might have happened to William when he was 20 kilometres from home.

....

.... (1 mark)

b) At what speed did William travel in the first 20 kilometres?

.... (2 marks)

William stayed at the market for 30 minutes and then cycled home at 25 kilometres per hour.

c) Complete the distance–time graph to show this information. (3 marks)

d) At approximately what time did William arrive home? .... (1 mark)

Score   / 7

How well did you do?

1–4 marks   Try again
5–8 marks   Getting there
9–13 marks   Good work
14–17 marks   Excellent!

TOTAL SCORE   / 17

For more information on this topic see pages 42–43 of your Success Guide.

SYMMETRY AND CONSTRUCTIONS

A

Choose just one answer, a, b, c or d.

Questions 1–5 relate to these diagrams.

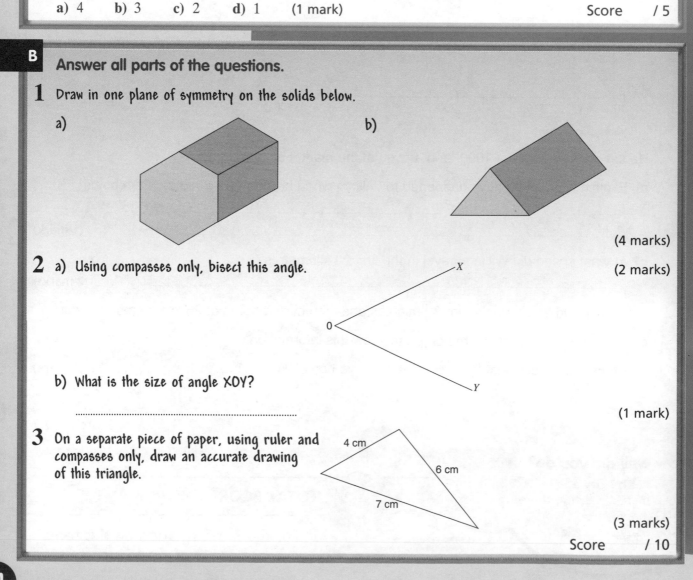

A B C D

1 What is the order of rotational symmetry of shape A?

a) 4   b) 2   c) 3   d) 1   (1 mark)

2 How many planes of symmetry does shape D have?

a) 5   b) 4   c) 2   d) 3   (1 mark)

3 How many lines of symmetry does shape B have?

a) 4   b) 3   c) 2   d) 1   (1 mark)

4 What is the order of rotational symmetry of shape C?

a) 1   b) 3   c) 2   d) 4   (1 mark)

5 How many lines of symmetry does shape C have?

a) 4   b) 2   c) 3   d) 1   (1 mark)

Score   / 5

B

Answer all parts of the questions.

1 Draw in one plane of symmetry on the solids below.

a)

b)

(4 marks)

2 a) Using compasses only, bisect this angle.   (2 marks)

X

O

Y

b) What is the size of angle XOY?

....

(1 mark)

3 On a separate piece of paper, using ruler and compasses only, draw an accurate drawing of this triangle.

4 cm

6 cm

7 cm

(3 marks)

Score   / 10

44

C These are GCSE style questions. Answer all parts of the questions. Show your workings (on separate paper if necessary) and include the correct units in your answers.

1 **a)** Draw the lines of symmetry on the rectangle below.

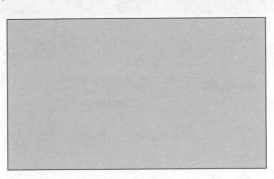

(2 marks)

b) What is the order of rotational symmetry of the rectangle?

.... (1 mark)

2 The diagram shows a prism. Draw one plane of symmetry of the prism on the diagram.

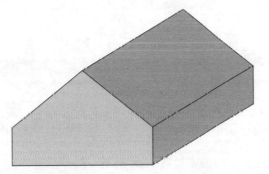

(2 marks)

3 Showing construction lines, draw accurately the perpendicular bisector of this line.

A _____ B

(2 marks)

Score   / 7

How well did you do?

1–6 marks   Try again
7–11 marks   Getting there
12–17 marks   Good work
18–22 marks   Excellent!

TOTAL SCORE   / 22

For more information on this topic see pages 48–49 of your Success Guide.

ANGLES

A

Choose just one answer, a, b, c or d.

1 What is the name given to an angle of size 72°?
a) acute
b) obtuse
c) reflex
d) right angle   (1 mark)

2 When shapes tessellate, the angles at the point at which they meet add up to this angle.
a) 180°   b) 90°
c) 360°   d) 270°   (1 mark)

3 Two angles in a scalene triangle are 104° and 39°. What is the size of the third angle?
a) 217°   b) 37°
c) 57°   d) 157°   (1 mark)

4 In the diagram below, what is the size of angle *a*?

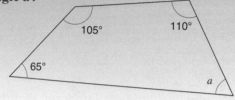

a) 90°   b) 80°
c) 75°   d) 100°   (1 mark)

5 The size of the exterior angle of a regular polygon is 20°. How many sides does the polygon have?
a) 18   b) 15
c) 10   d) 20   (1 mark)

Score   / 5

B

Answer all parts of the questions.

1 Here are the sizes of some angles, written on card.

148° 60° 91° 63° 154° 65° 68°

Match the correct card to the missing angle n in each of the diagrams.

a)
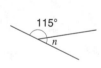
n = ...
(1 mark)

b)

n = ...
(1 mark)

c)
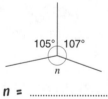
n = ...
(1 mark)

d)
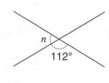
n = ...
(1 mark)

e)

n = ...
(1 mark)

f)
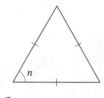
n = ...
(1 mark)

g)
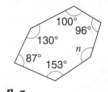
n = ...
(2 marks)

2 On the grid, draw six more shapes to continue this tessellation.

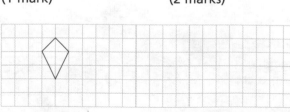

(2 marks)

Score   / 10

46

C

These are GCSE style questions. Answer all parts of the questions. Show your workings (on separate paper if necessary) and include the correct units in your answers.

1 In the diagram, AB is vertical and BDE is a horizontal straight line.

BC = BD, CF is parallel to BDE.

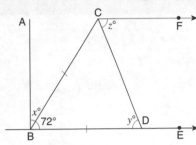

a) i) Work out the size of the angle marked $x°$.

....° (2 marks)

ii) Give a reason for your answer.

....

.... (2 marks)

b) i) Work out the size of the angle marked $y°$.

....°

ii) Give a reason for your answer.

....

.... (2 marks)

c) i) Work out the size of the angle marked $z°$.

....°

ii) Give a reason for your answer.

....

.... (2 marks)

2 The diagram shows a hexagon.

Find the size of the angle marked $x°$.

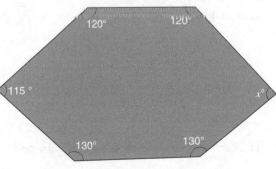

....° (4 marks)

Score   / 12

How well did you do?

1–7 marks   Try again
8–13 marks   Getting there
14–21 marks   Good work
22–27 marks   Excellent!

TOTAL SCORE   / 25

For more information on this topic
see pages 50–51 of your Success Guide.

BEARINGS AND SCALE DRAWINGS

A

Choose just one answer, a, b, c or d.

1 The bearing of P from Q is 050°. What is the bearing of Q from P?
a) 130°
b) 50°
c) 230°
d) 310°   (1 mark)

2 The bearing of R from S is 130°. What is the bearing of S from R?
a) 310°
b) 230°
c) 050°
d) 200°   (1 mark)

3 The bearing of A from B is 240°. What is the bearing of B from A?
a) 120°
b) 60°
c) 320°
d) 060°   (1 mark)

4 The length of a car park is 25 metres. A scale diagram of the car park is being drawn to a scale of 1 cm to 5 metres. What is the length of the car park on the scale diagram?
a) 500 mm
b) 5 cm
c) 50 cm
d) 5 m   (1 mark)

Score   / 4

B

Answer all parts of the questions.

1 The scale on a road map is 1 : 50 000. Two towns are 20 cm apart on the map. Work out the real distance, in km, between them.

.... km   (2 marks)

2 A ship sails on a bearing of 065° for 10 km. It then continues on a bearing of 120° for a further 15 km to a port (P).

a) On a separate piece of paper, draw, using a scale of 1 cm to 2 km, an accurate scale drawing of this information.

     (3 marks)

b) Measure on your diagram the direct distance between the start and the port (P).

.... km   (1 mark)

c) What is the bearing of port P from the starting point?

.... °   (1 mark)

3 Is this statement is true or false?

'The bearing of B from A is 060°'

....   (1 mark)

Score   / 8

C These are GCSE style questions. Answer all parts of the questions. Show your workings (on separate paper if necessary) and include the correct units in your answers.

1

Scale: 1 cm represents 50 m

The scale drawing shows the positions of points A, B, C and D. Point C is due east of point A.

a) Use measurements from the drawing to find these.

    i) The distance, in metres, of B from A   .... m   (1 mark)

    ii) The bearing of B from A   .... °   (2 marks)

    iii) The bearing of D from B   .... °   (2 marks)

b) Point E is 250 m from C on a bearing of 055°. Mark the position of point E on the diagram above.   (2 marks)

2 Here is a sketch of a triangle.

Use a scale of 1 cm to 2 m to make an accurate scale drawing of the triangle.

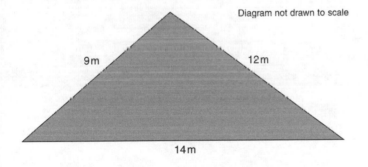

Diagram not drawn to scale

9 m   12 m

14 m

(3 marks)

Score   / 10

How well did you do?

1–4 marks	Try again
5–10 marks	Getting there
11–16 marks	Good work
17–22 marks	Excellent!

TOTAL SCORE   / 22

For more information on this topic see pages 52–53 of your Success Guide.

TRANSFORMATIONS 1

A

Choose just one answer, a, b, c or d.
Questions 1–4 refer to the artwork opposite.

1 What is the transformation that would map shape A onto shape B?
a) reflection   b) rotation
c) translation   d) enlargement   (1 mark)

2 What is the transformation that would map shape A onto shape C?
a) reflection   b) rotation
c) translation   d) enlargement   (1 mark)

3 What is the transformation that would map shape A onto shape D?
a) reflection   b) rotation
c) translation   d) enlargement   (1 mark)

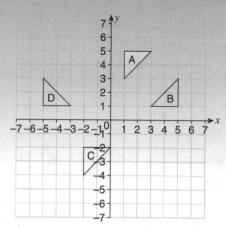

4 What special name is given to triangles A, B, C and D?
a) enlargement   b) congruent
c) translation   d) similar   (1 mark)

Score   / 4

B

Answer all parts of the questions.

1 On the grid below carry out the following transformations.

a) Reflect shape A in the y axis.
Call the shape R.

b) Rotate shape A 90° clockwise, about (0, 0)
Call the shape S.

c) Translate shape A by the vector $\begin{pmatrix} -3 \\ 4 \end{pmatrix}$
Call the shape T.

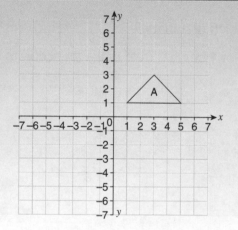

(3 marks)

2 All the following shapes are either a reflection, rotation or translation of object P. State the transformation that has taken place for each of the following.

a) P is transformed to A ....

b) P is transformed to B ....

c) P is transformed to C ....

d) P is transformed to D ....

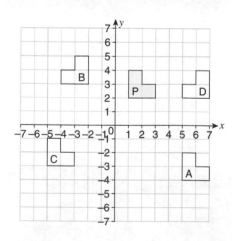

(4 marks)

Score   / 7

50

C These are GCSE style questions. Answer all parts of the questions. Show your workings (on separate paper if necessary) and include the correct units in your answers.

1

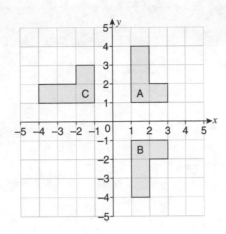

a) Describe fully the single transformation which takes shape A onto shape B.

....

.... (2 marks)

b) Describe fully the single transformation which takes shape A onto shape C.

....

.... (3 marks)

2

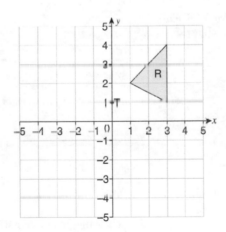

The triangle R has been drawn on the grid.

a) Rotate triangle R 90° clockwise about the point T (0, 1) and call the image P. (3 marks)

b) Translate triangle R by the vector $\begin{pmatrix} -4 \\ -3 \end{pmatrix}$ and call the image Q. (3 marks)

Score   / 11

How well did you do?

1–6 marks   Try again
7–10 marks   Getting there
11–16 marks   Good work
17–22 marks   Excellent!

TOTAL SCORE   / 22

For more information on this topic
see pages 54–55 of your Success Guide.

TRANSFORMATIONS 2

A Choose just one answer, a, b, c or d.
Questions 1–3 refer to the diagram opposite.

1 Shape P is enlarged to give shape Q. What is the scale factor of the enlargement?
   a) $\frac{1}{3}$ b) 2
   c) 3   d) $\frac{1}{2}$ (1 mark)

2 Shape Q is enlarged to give shape P. What is the scale factor of the enlargement?
   a) $\frac{1}{3}$ b) 2
   c) 3   d) $\frac{1}{2}$ (1 mark)

3 What are the coordinates of the centre of enlargement?
   a) (3, –2)   b) (–2, 3)
   c) (–3, 4)   d) (0, 0)   (1 mark)

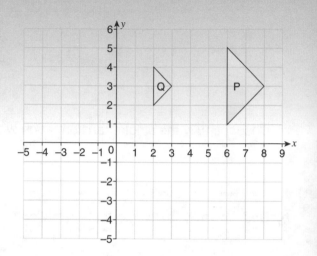

Score   / 3

B Answer all parts of the questions.

1 Draw an enlargement of shape R, with centre O and scale factor 3. Call the new shape P.

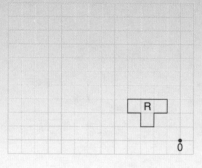

(3 marks)

2 The diagram shows the position of three shapes A, B and C.

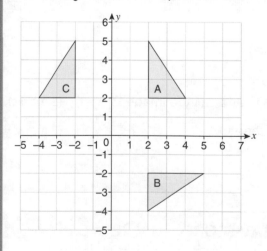

a) Describe the transformation which moves A onto C.
....
.... (2 marks)

b) Describe the transformation which moves A onto B.
....
.... (2 marks)

c) Describe the transformation which moves B onto C.
....
.... (2 marks)

Score   / 9

52

C

These are GCSE style questions. Answer all parts of the questions. Show your workings (on separate paper if necessary) and include the correct units in your answers.

1 a) Draw an enlargement of the shape.

Use a scale factor of 2.

Call the enlarged shape A.

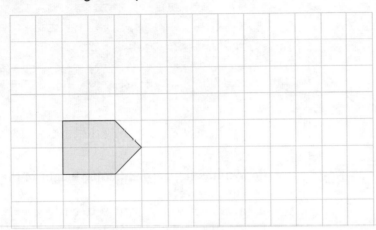

(2 marks)

b) If the area of the original shape is 5 cm², what is the area of the enlarged shape?

.... cm²

(1 mark)

2 Enlarge triangle N by a scale factor of $\frac{1}{3}$ with centre R (–6, 7)

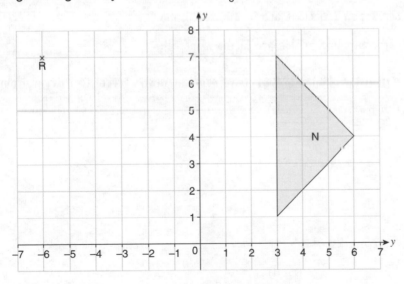

(3 marks)

Score   / 6

How well did you do?

1–3 marks   Try again
4–8 marks   Getting there
9–13 marks   Good work
14–18 marks Excellent!

TOTAL SCORE   / 18

For more information on this topic see pages 56–57 of your Success Guide.

SIMILARITY

A

Choose just one answer, a, b, c or d.

1 These two shapes are similar. What is the size of angle *x*?

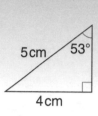 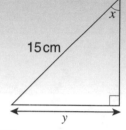

5 cm 53° 4 cm

15 cm *x* *y*

a) 90° b) 47°
c) 53° d) 50° (1 mark)

2 What is the length of *y* in the triangles above?
a) 14 cm b) 12 cm
c) 8 cm d) 16 cm (1 mark)

3 These two shapes are similar. What is the radius of the smaller cone?

Diagrams not drawn to scale

5 cm 4 cm 11.45 cm *y*
⊢—⊣ = *x* ⊢—⊣ = 7.152 cm

a) 2 cm b) 3.12 cm
c) 4 cm d) 5 cm (1 mark)

4 What is the perpendicular height of the larger cone above?
a) 12 cm b) 9.16 cm
c) 10.47 cm d) 10 cm (1 mark)

Score / 4

B

Answer all parts of the questions.

1 Decide whether these statements are true or false.

a) If two shapes are similar, corresponding sides are in the same ratio. ....

b) If two shapes are similar, corresponding angles are in the same ratio. .... (2 marks)

 2 Calculate the lengths marked *n* in these similar shapes. Give your answers correct to 1 decimal place.

a)

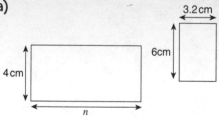

3.2 cm
6 cm
4 cm
n

n = ... cm (2 marks)

b)

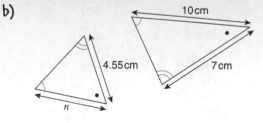

10 cm
4.55 cm 7 cm
n

n = ... cm (2 marks)

c)

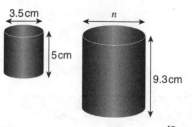

3.5 cm *n*
5 cm
9.3 cm

n = ... cm (2 marks)

d)

 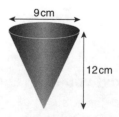

5.5 cm 9 cm
n 12 cm

n = ... cm (2 marks)

Score / 10

C These are GCSE style questions. Answer all parts of the questions. Show your workings (on separate paper if necessary) and include the correct units in your answers.

1

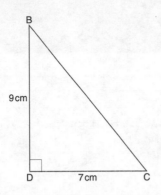

Diagrams not drawn to scale

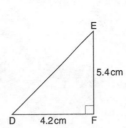

Are these two triangles similar? Give reasons for your answer.

....

.... (2 marks)

2 In the diagram MN is parallel to YZ.

YMX and ZNX are straight lines.

XM = 5.1 cm, XY = 9.5 cm,
XN = 6.3 cm, YZ = 6.8 cm.

∠YXZ = 29°, ∠XZY = 68°.

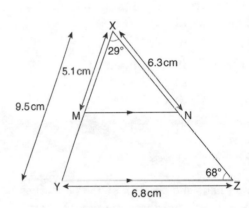

Diagram not drawn to scale

a) i) Calculate the size of angle XMN.

....° (1 mark)

ii) Explain how you obtained your answer.

....

.... (1 mark)

b) Calculate the length of MN.

.... cm (2 marks)

c) Calculate the length of XZ.

.... cm (2 marks)

Score   / 8

How well did you do?

1–6 marks   Try again
7–11 marks   Getting there
12–16 marks   Good work
17–22 marks   Excellent!

TOTAL SCORE   / 22

For more information on this topic see page 58 of your Success Guide.

LOCI AND COORDINATES IN 3D

SHAPE, SPACE AND MEASURES

A Choose just one answer, a, b, c or d.

1 What shape will be formed if the locus of all the points from a fixed point P is drawn?
a) rectangle　　　b) square
c) circle　　　　d) kite　　　　(1 mark)

Questions 2–5 refer to the diagram opposite.

2 What are the coordinates of point A?
a) (4, 3, 1)　　　b) (4, 3, 0)
c) (0, 3, 1)　　　d) (4, 0, 1)　　(1 mark)

3 What are the coordinates of point B?
a) (0, 3, 1)　　　b) (0, 0, 0)
c) (4, 3, 0)　　　d) (0, 3, 0)　　(1 mark)

4 What are the coordinates of point C?
a) (0, 3, 1)　　　b) (4, 3, 1)
c) (4, 0, 0)　　　d) (4, 3, 0)　　(1 mark)

5 What are the coordinates of point D?
a) (4, 3, 0)　　　b) (4, 3, 1)
c) (0, 0, 0)　　　d) (0, 3, 0)　　(1 mark)

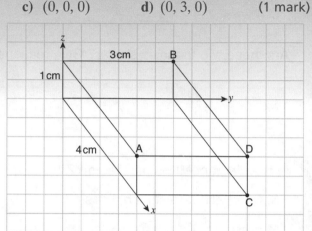

Score　　/ 5

B Answer all parts of the questions.

1 The diagram shows the position of the post office (P), the hospital (H) and the school (S). Robert lives within 4 miles of the hospital, under 5 miles from the post office and fewer than 8 miles from the school. Show by shading the area where Robert can live. Use a scale of 1 cm = 2 miles.

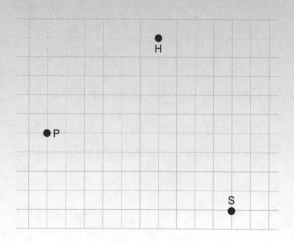

(4 marks)

2 The diagram shows a solid. Complete the coordinates for each of the vertices listed below.

R = (.... , ... , ...)

S = (.... , ... , ...)

T = (.... , ... , ...)

U = (.... , ... , ...)

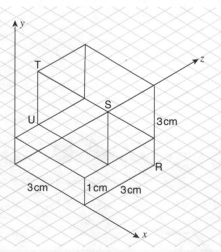

(4 marks)

Score　　/ 8

56

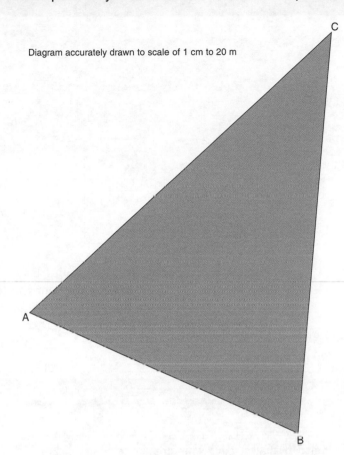

C This is a GCSE style question. Answer all parts of the question. Show all your workings (on separate paper if necessary) and include the correct units in your answers.

1 In this question you should use ruler and compasses only for the constructions.

Diagram accurately drawn to scale of 1 cm to 20 m

Triangle ABC is an adventure playground, drawn to a scale of 1 cm to 20 m.

a) On the diagram, draw accurately the locus of the points which are 100 m from C. *(2 marks)*

b) On the diagram, draw accurately the locus of the points which are the same distance from A as they are from C. *(2 marks)*

c) P is an ice cream kiosk inside the adventure playground.

P is the same distance from A as it is from C.

P is the same distance from AC as it is from AB.

On the diagram, mark the point P clearly with a cross.

Label it with the letter P. *(3 marks)*

Score   / 7

How well did you do?

1–4 marks   Try again
5–9 marks   Getting there
10–14 marks   Good work
15–20 marks   Excellent!

TOTAL SCORE   / 20

For more information on this topic see page 59 of your Success Guide.

PYTHAGORAS' THEOREM

A Choose just one answer, a, b, c or d.

1 What is the name of the longest side of a right-angled triangle?

a) hypo   b) hippopotomus
c) crocodile   d) hypotenuse   (1 mark)

2 Calculate the missing length y of this triangle.

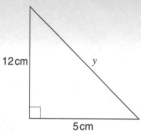

12cm

y

5cm

a) 169 cm   b) 13 cm
c) 17 cm   d) 84.5 cm   (1 mark)

3 Calculate the missing length y of this triangle.
a) 13.2 cm   b) 5 cm
c) 25 cm   d) 625 cm   (1 mark)

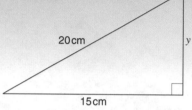

20cm y

15cm

4 Point A has coordinates (1, 4), point B has coordinates (4, 10). What are the coordinates of the midpoint of the line AB?
a) (5, 14)   b) (3, 6)
c) (2.5, 7)   d) (1.5, 3)   (1 mark)

Score   / 4

B Answer all parts of the questions.

1 Calculate the missing lengths of these right-angled triangles. Give your answer to 3 significant figures, where appropriate.

a)

9cm n

12cm

n = ...

(2 marks)

b)

n

15.2cm   8.5cm

n = ...

(2 marks)

c)

n

12.1cm   9cm

n = ...

(2 marks)

d)

31cm n

18.9cm

n = ...

(2 marks)

2 Molly says, 'The angle x in this triangle is 90°.' Explain how Molly knows this without measuring the size of the angle.

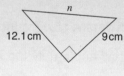

12cm   13cm

$x°$

5cm

....

....

(2 marks)

3 Colin says, 'The length of this line is $\sqrt{45}$ units and the coordinates of the midpoint are (3.5, 8).' Decide whether these statements are true or false. Give an explanation for your answer.

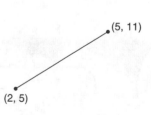

(5, 11)

(2, 5)

....

....

(2 marks)

Score   / 12

C

These are GCSE style questions. Answer all parts of the questions. Show your workings (on separate paper if necessary) and include the correct units in your answers.

1 ABC is a right-angled triangle.

AB = 5 cm, BC = 6 cm.

Calculate the length of AC.

Leave your answer in surd form.

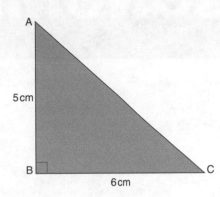

.... cm

(3 marks)

2 Calculate the length of the diagonal of this rectangle. Give your answer to one decimal place.

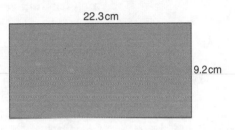

.... cm

(3 marks)

3 Calculate the perpendicular height of the isosceles triangle. Give your answer to one decimal place.

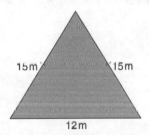

.... cm

(3 marks)

4 Calculate the length of AB in this diagram.
Leave your answer in surd form.

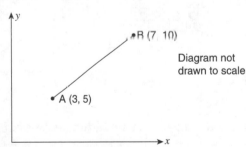

Diagram not drawn to scale

.... cm

(3 marks)

Score   / 12

How well did you do?

1–7 marks	Try again
8–14 marks	Getting there
15–21 marks	Good work
22–28 marks	Excellent!

TOTAL SCORE   / 28

For more information on this topic see pages 60–61 of your Success Guide.

TRIGONOMETRY 1

A

Choose just one answer, a, b, c or d.
Questions 1–5 refer to this diagram.

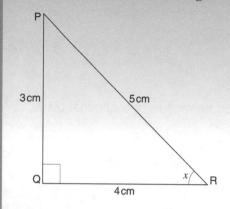

1 Which length is the opposite to angle x?
  a) PQ   **b)** PR   **c)** QR   **d)** RX   (1 mark)

2 Which length of the triangle is the hypotenuse?
  a) PQ   **b)** PR   **c)** QR   **d)** RX   (1 mark)

3 Which fraction represents tan x?
  a) $\frac{3}{5}$ **b)** $\frac{4}{3}$ **c)** $\frac{4}{5}$ **d)** $\frac{3}{4}$ (1 mark)

4 Which fraction represents sin x?
  a) $\frac{3}{5}$ **b)** $\frac{4}{3}$ **c)** $\frac{5}{3}$ **d)** $\frac{4}{5}$ (1 mark)

5 Which fraction represents cos x?
  a) $\frac{3}{5}$ **b)** $\frac{3}{4}$ **c)** $\frac{4}{5}$ **d)** $\frac{5}{4}$ (1 mark)

Score   / 5

B

Answer all parts of the questions.

1 Label the sides of these triangles (with opp, adj and hyp) with respect to angle θ.

(3 marks)

2 Choose a card for each of the missing lengths n on the triangles. The lengths have been rounded to 1 decimal place.

| 6.3 cm | 6.7 cm | 13.8 cm | 5 cm | 14.9 cm |

a)   **b)** 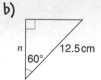   **c)** 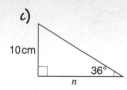   **d)** 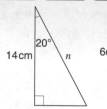   **e)**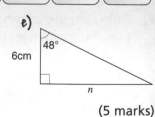

(5 marks)

3 Work out the missing angle x in the diagrams below. **Give your answers to 1 decimal place.**

a) 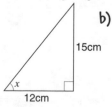   **b)**    **c)**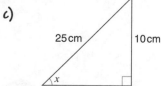

x = ... ° x = ... ° x = ... °

(2 marks)   (2 marks)   (2 marks)

Score   / 14

C These are GCSE style questions. Answer all parts of the questions. Show your workings (on separate paper if necessary) and include the correct units in your answers.

1 RS and SU are two sides of a rectangle.

T is a point on SU.

SU is 50 cm.

ST is 18 cm.

Angle STU is 40°.

Calculate the width of the rectangle.

Give your answer correct to the nearest centimetre.

.... cm

(3 marks)

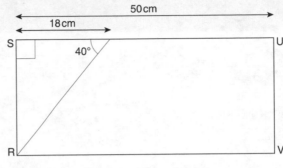

Diagram not drawn to scale

2 The diagram shows two triangles PQR and QRS.

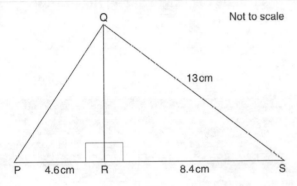

Not to scale

a) Calculate the length of QR.

.... cm   (2 marks)

b) Calculate angle QPR.

.....................................°   (3 marks)

3 The diagram shows a right-angled triangle ABC.

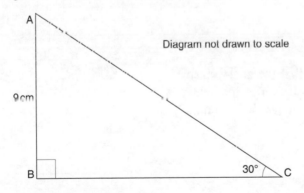

Diagram not drawn to scale

Calculate the length of AC.

.... cm

(3 marks)

Score   / 11

How well did you do?

1–7 marks   Try again
8–13 marks   Getting there
14–21 marks Good work
22–30 marks Excellent!

TOTAL SCORE   / 30

For more information on this topic see pages 62–63 of your Success Guide.

TRIGONOMETRY 2

A Choose just one answer, a, b, c or d.

Questions 1–3 refer to this diagram.

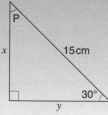

Question 4 and 5 refer to this diagram.

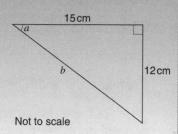

Not to scale

 1 Calculate the value of *x*.
  a) 13 cm   b) 8.7 cm
  c) 7.5 cm   d) 10 cm   (1 mark)

 2 Calculate the value of *y*.
  a) 13 cm   b) 8.7 cm
  c) 7.5 cm   d) 10 cm   (1 mark)

3 Which fraction represents cos *P*?
  a) $\frac{13}{15}$ b) $\frac{3}{4}$
  c) $\frac{3}{5}$ d) $\frac{1}{2}$ (1 mark)

4 Calculate the size of angle *a* to the nearest degree.
  a) 53°   b) 45°   c) 39°   d) 37°
                    (1 mark)

5 Calculate the length of *b* to the nearest centimetre.
  a) 9 cm   b) 19 cm
  c) 29 cm   d) 16 cm   (1 mark)

Score   / 5

B Answer all parts of the questions.

1 A ship sails 20 Km due north and then 50 Km due east. What is the bearing of the finishing point from the starting point?

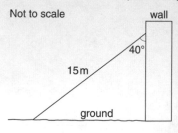

50 km   finish

20 km

start   Not to scale

Bearing .... °   (2 marks)

2 A ladder rests against a wall in such a way that the angle which the ladder makes with the wall is 40°. If the length of the ladder is 15 metres, calculate the height of the ladder above the ground. Give your answer to 1 decimal place.

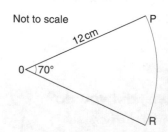

Not to scale   wall
            40°
15 m
        ground

.... m   (3 marks)

3 The diagram represents the sector of a circle with centre O and radius 12 cm. Angle POR equals 70°.

Calculate the length of the straight line PR.

Not to scale   P
        12 cm
O 70°
            R

.... cm   (3 marks)

Score   / 8

C These are GCSE style questions. Answer all parts of the questions. Show your workings (on separate paper if necessary) and include the correct units in your answers.

1 The diagram shows the position of some towns: Swanley is due north of Toole.

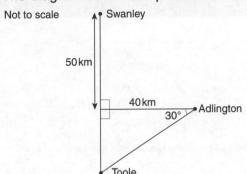

a) Calculate the direct distance between Swanley and Adlington. Give your answer to the nearest kilometre.

....
.... (2 marks)

b) Calculate the total distance between Swanley and Toole. Give your answer to the nearest kilometre.

....
.... (3 marks)

c) Calculate the bearing of Adlington from Swanley. Give your answer to the nearest degree.

....
.... (3 marks)

2 The diagram shows a triangle PQR.

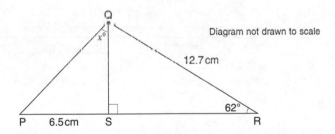

PS = 6.5 cm, QR = 12.7 cm and angle QRS = 62°.

Calculate the size of the angle marked $x°$.

Give your answer correct to 1 decimal place. .... (5 marks)

Score   / 13

How well did you do?

1–6 marks   Try again
7–13 marks   Getting there
14–20 marks   Good work
21–26 marks   Excellent!

TOTAL SCORE   / 26

For more information on this topic see page 64 of your Success Guide.

ANGLE PROPERTIES OF CIRCLES

A

Choose just one answer, a, b, c or d.
Questions 1–5 refer to the diagrams drawn below.

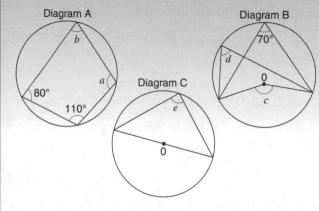

Diagram A

Diagram B

Diagram C

1 In diagram A, what is the size of angle *a*?
a) 80°   b) 110°
c) 100°   d) 70°   (1 mark)

2 In diagram A, what is the size of angle *b*?
a) 70°   b) 110°
c) 100°   d) 80°   (1 mark)

3 In diagram B, what is the size of angle *c*?
a) 35°   b) 70°
c) 100°   d) 140°   (1 mark)

4 In diagram B, what is the size of angle *d*?
a) 70°   b) 35°
c) 100°   d) 140°   (1 mark)

5 In diagram C, what is the size of angle *e*?
a) 100°   b) 45°
c) 90°   d) 110°   (1 mark)

Score   / 5

B

Answer all parts of the questions.

1 Some angles are written on cards.
Match the missing angles in the diagrams
below with the correct card. O represents
the centre of the circle.

| 50° | 60° | 82° | 65° | 18° |

a)

b)
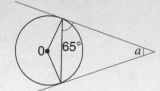

c)

d)
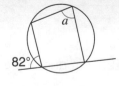

(5 marks)

2 John says that 'angle a is 42°'.

Explain whether John is correct.

e)

....

....

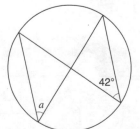

(1 mark)

Score   / 6

64

C These are GCSE style questions. Answer all parts of the questions. Show your workings (on separate paper if necessary) and include the correct units in your answers.

1

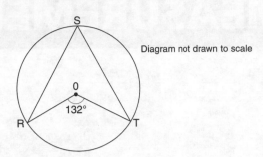

Diagram not drawn to scale

R, S and T are points on the circumference of a circle with centre O.

a) Find angle RST.

.... ⁰ (1 mark)

b) Give a reason for your answer.

....

.... (2 marks)

2

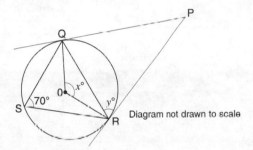

Diagram not drawn to scale

PQ and PR are tangents to a circle centre O.

Point S is a point on the circumference.

Angle RSQ is 70°.

a) Find angle ROQ, marked x° in the diagram.

.... ⁰ (2 marks)

b) Find the size of angle PRQ, marked y° in the diagram.

....

....

....

.... (4 marks)

Score   / 9

How well did you do?

1–2 marks   Try again
3–6 marks   Getting there
7–12 marks Good work
13–20 marks Excellent!

TOTAL SCORE   / 20

For more information on this topic see page 65 of your Success Guide.

MEASURES AND MEASUREMENT

A

Choose just one answer, a, b, c or d.

1 What is 2 500 g in kilograms?
a) 25 kg
b) 2.5 kg
c) 0.25 kg
d) 250 kg   (1 mark)

2 Approximately how many pounds are in 4 kg?
a) 6.9
b) 12.4
c) 7.7
d) 8.8   (1 mark)

3 Jessica is 165 cm tall to the nearest cm. What is the lower limit of her height?
a) 164.5 cm
b) 165.5 cm
c) 165 cm
d) 164.9 cm   (1 mark)

4 What is the volume of a piece of wood with a density of 680 kg/m^3 and a mass of 34 kg?
a) 0.5 m^3
b) 20 m^3
c) 2 m^3
d) 0.05 m^3 (1 mark)

5 A car travels for two and a half hours at a speed of 42 mph. How far does the car travel?
a) 96 miles
b) 100 miles
c) 105 miles
d) 140 miles   (1 mark)

Score   / 5

B

Answer all parts of the questions.

1 Complete the statements below.

a) 8 km = ... m

b) 3 250 g = ... kg

c) 7 tonnes = ... kg

d) 52 cm = ... m

e) 2.7 l = ... ml

e) 262 cm = ... km   (6 marks)

2 Two towns are approximately 20 km apart. How many miles is this?

.... (1 mark)

3 A recipe uses 600 g of flour. Approximately how many pounds is this?

.... (1 mark)

4 A field is 47 metres long to the nearest metre. Write down the upper and lower limits of the length of the field.

.... (2 marks)

5 Giovanni drove 200 miles in 3 hours and 45 minutes. At what average speed did he travel?

.... (2 marks)

6 What is the density of a toy if its mass is 200 g and its volume is 2 000 cm^3?

.... (2 marks)

Score   / 14

C These are GCSE style questions. Answer all parts of the questions. Show your workings (on separate paper if necessary) and include the correct units in your answers.

1 a) Change 8 kilograms into pounds.

....pounds

(2 marks)

b) Change 30 miles into kilometres.

....kilometres

(2 marks)

2 Two solids each have a volume of 2.5m³.

The density of solid A is 320 kg per m³.

The density of solid B is 288 kg per m³.

Calculate the difference in the masses of the solids. ....kg

(3 marks)

3 Amy took part in a sponsored walk.

She walked from the school to the park and back.

The distance from the school to the park is 8 km.

a) Amy walked from the school to the park at an average speed of 5 km/h.

Find the time she took to walk from the school to the park.

....

(2 marks)

b) Her average speed for the return journey was 4 km/h.

Calculate her average speed for the whole journey.

....

(4 marks)

4 The length of the rectangle is 12.1 cm to the nearest mm.

12.1 cm

6 cm

The width of the rectangle is 6 cm to the nearest cm.

Write down the lower limits for the length and width of the rectangle.

Length   .... cm

Width   .... cm

(2 marks)

Score   / 15

How well did you do?

1–11 marks   Try again
12–19 marks   Getting there
20–27 marks   Good work
28–34 marks   Excellent!

TOTAL SCORE   / 34

For more information on this topic see pages 66–67 of your Success Guide.

AREA OF 2D SHAPES

A

Choose just one answer, a, b, c or d.

1 What is the area of this triangle?

8cm

15cm

a) 60 mm²
b) 120 cm²
c) 60 cm²
d) 46 cm²   (1 mark)

2 What is the approximate circumference of a circle of radius 4 cm?

a) 25.1 cm²
b) 50.3 cm
c) 12.6 cm
d) 25.1 cm   (1 mark)

3 Change 50 000 cm² into m².

a) 500 m²
b) 5 m²
c) 0.5 m²
d) 50 m²   (1 mark)

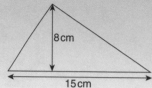 **4** What is the area of this circle?

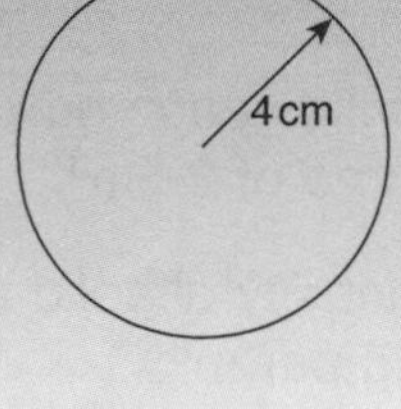

4cm

a) 25.1 cm²
b) 55 cm²
c) 12.6 cm²
d) 50.3 cm²
(1 mark)

5 If the area of a rectangle is 20 cm² and its width is 2.5 cm, what is the length of the rectangle?

a) 9 cm   b) 8 cm   c) 7.5 cm   d) 2.5 cm
(1 mark)

Score   / 5

B

Answer all parts of the questions.

1 For each of the diagrams below, decide whether the area given is true or false.

a)

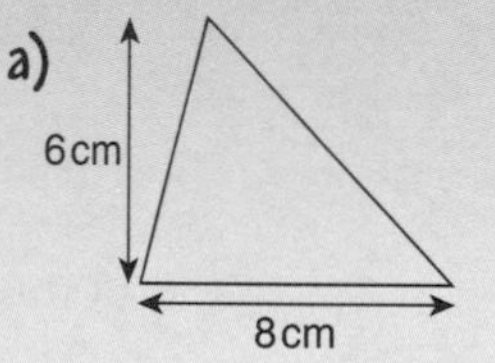

6cm

8cm

Area = 48 cm² ....
(1 mark)

b)

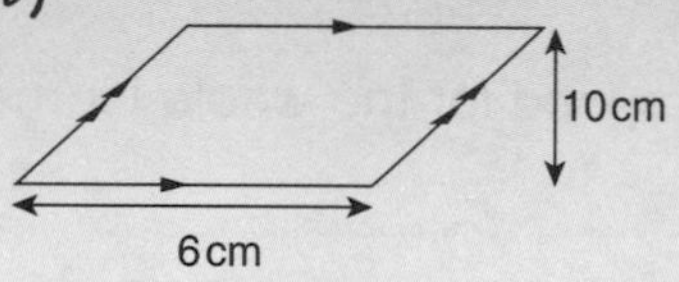

10cm

6cm

Area = 60 cm² ....
(1 mark)

c)

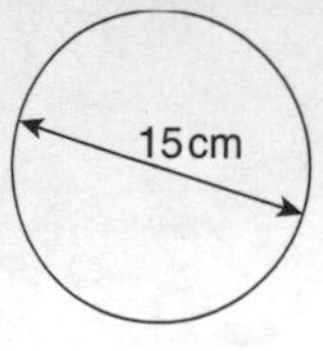

15cm

Area = 177 cm² ....
(1 mark)

d)

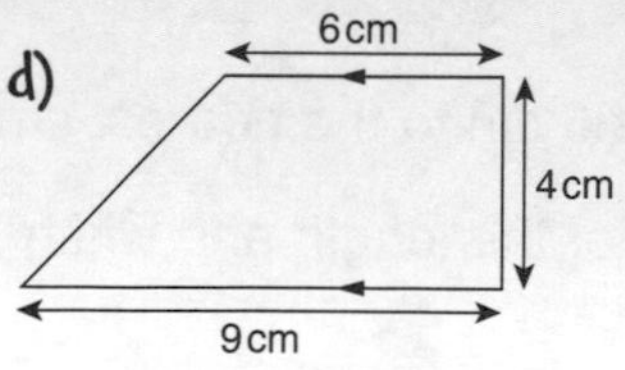

6cm

4cm

9cm

Area = 108 cm² ....
(1 mark)

2 Calculate the perimeter of this shape.

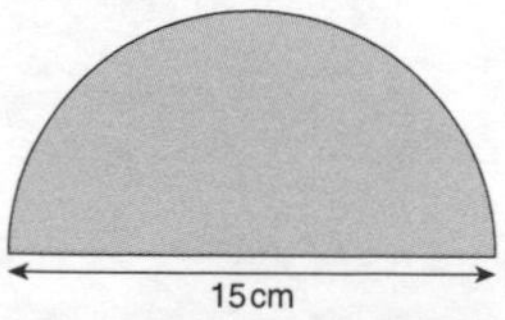

.... cm

15cm

(3 marks)

3 Calculate the area of the shaded region.

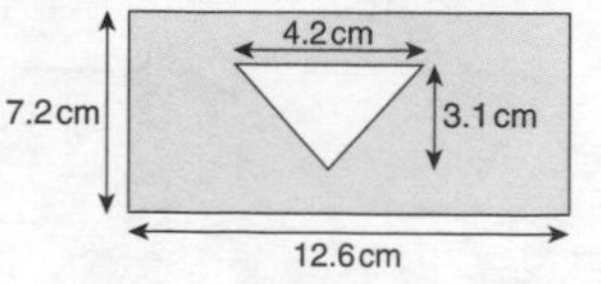

7.2cm

4.2cm

3.1cm

12.6cm

.... cm²

(3 marks)

Score   / 10

C These are GCSE style questions. Answer all parts of the questions. Show your workings (on separate paper if necessary) and include the correct units in your answers.

1 Work out the area of the shape shown in the diagram.

State the units with your answer.

....

....

....

....

....

....

15cm

8cm

5cm

9cm

Diagram not drawn to scale

(5 marks)

2 Calculate the perimeter of the shape shown in the diagram.

Give your answer to 3 significant figures.

....

....

....

....

....

.... cm

10cm

(3 marks)

3 The area of a circular sewing pattern is 200 cm^2

Calculate the diameter of the sewing pattern. Give your answer correct to the nearest centimetre.

....

.... cm   (4 marks)

4 Calculate the area of the shape.

State the units with your answer.

....

....

....

....

13.8cm

7.2cm

19.6cm

(3 marks)

Score   / 15

How well did you do?

1–8 marks   Try again
9–14 marks   Getting there
15–22 marks   Good work
23–30 marks   Excellent!

TOTAL SCORE   /30

For more information on this topic see pages 68–69 of your Success Guide.

VOLUME OF 3D SHAPES

A

Choose just one answer, a, b, c or d.

1 What is the volume of this cuboid?
a) 30 cm³
b) 16 cm³
c) 300 mm³
d) 15 cm³

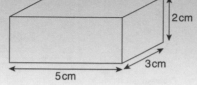

(1 mark)

2 What is the volume of this prism?
a) 64 cm³
b) 240 cm³
c) 120 cm³
d) 20 cm³

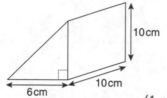

(1 mark)

3 The volume of a cuboid is 20 cm³. If its height is 1 cm and its width is 4 cm, what is its length?
a) 5 cm   b) 10 cm
c) 15 cm   d) 8 cm   (1 mark)

4 A cube of volume 2 cm³ is enlarged by a scale factor of 3. What is the volume of the enlarged cube?
a) 6 cm³   b) 27 cm³
c) 54 cm³   d) 18 cm³   (1 mark)

5 If p and q represent lengths, decide what the formula $\frac{3}{5}\pi p^2 q$ shows.
a) circumference   b) length
c) area   d) volume   (1 mark)

Score   / 5

B

Answer all parts of the questions.

1 Emily says: 'The volume of this prism is 345.6 m³'

Decide whether Emily is correct. Show working out to justify your answer.

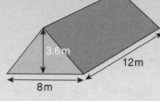

....

....   (1 mark)

2 Calculate the volume of the cylinder, clearly stating your units.

....   (2 marks)

3 If the volume of both solids is the same, work out the height of the cylinder to 1 decimal place.

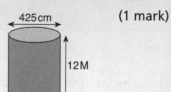

....   (4 marks)

4 Lucy said that 'The volume of a sphere is given by the formula V = 4πr²'. Explain why she cannot be correct.

....   (1 mark)

Score   / 8

C These are GCSE style questions. Answer all parts of the questions. Show your workings (on separate paper if necessary) and include the correct units in your answers.

1 A cube has a surface area of 96 cm². Work out the volume of the cube.

....cm (4 marks)

2 A door wedge is in the shape of a prism with cross section VWXY.

VW = 7 cm, VY = 0.15 m, WX = 9 cm.

The width of the door wedge is 0.08 m.

a) Calculate the volume of the door wedge.

....cm³ (3 marks)

b) What is the volume of the door wedge in m³?

....m³ (1 mark)

3 The volume of this cylinder is 250 cm³.

The height of the cylinder is 8 cm.

Calculate the radius of the cylinder giving your answer to 1 decimal place.

.... cm (3 marks)

4 Here are three expressions.

Expression	Length	Area	Volume
$4r^2p$			
$3\pi\sqrt{r^2} + p^2$			
$\dfrac{4\pi r^2}{3p}$			

r and *p* are lengths.

Put a tick in the correct column to show whether the expression can be used for length, area or volume.   (3 marks)

5 The volume of a cube is 141 cm³.

Each length of the cube is enlarged by a scale factor of 3. What is the volume of the enlarged cube?

.... cm³ (2 marks)

Score   / 14

How well did you do?

1–7 marks   Try again
8–14 marks   Getting there
15–22 marks   Good work
23–29 marks   Excellent!

TOTAL SCORE   / 29

For more information on this topic see pages 70–71 of your Success Guide.

COLLECTING DATA

A **Choose just one answer, a, b, c, or d.**

1 What is the name given to data you
collect yourself?
a) continuous
b) primary
c) secondary
d) discrete (1 mark)

2 Data which is usually obtained by counting
is said to be this type of data.
a) continuous
b) primary
c) secondary
d) discrete (1 mark)

3 This type of data changes from one category
to the next.
a) continuous
b) primary
c) secondary
d) discrete (1 mark)

4 This type of data gives a word as an answer.
a) quantitative
b) qualitative
c) continuous
d) discrete (1 mark)

Score / 4

B **Answer all parts of the questions.**

1 Hannah and Thomas are collecting some data on the types of books read by students.

Draw a suitable data collecting sheet for this information.

(3 marks)

2 Imran and Annabelle are designing a survey to use in the school. One of their questions is shown below.

How much time do you spend doing homework per night?

| 0–1 hrs | 1–2 hrs | 2–3 hrs | 3–4 hrs |

What is the problem with this question? Rewrite the question so that it is improved.

....

....

.... (2 marks)

3 Emily decides to carry out a survey on how much football people watch on television.

She decides to ask 50 men outside a football ground on Saturday afternoon. Explain why her
results will be biased.

....

.... (2 marks)

Score / 7

C These are GCSE style questions. Answer all parts of the questions. Show your workings (on separate paper if necessary) and include the correct units in your answers.

1 Amy is going to carry out a survey to record information about the colour of vehicles passing the school gate.

In the space below, draw a suitable data collection sheet that Amy could use.

(3 marks)

2 Mrs Robinson is going to sell chocolate bars at the school tuck shop. She wants to know what type of chocolate bars pupils like. Design a suitable questionnaire she could use.

(2 marks)

3 Robert is conducting a survey into television habits. One of the questions in his survey is: 'Do you watch a lot of television?'.

His friend Jessica tells him that it is not a very good question. Write down two ways in which Robert could improve the question.

....

....

(2 marks)

Score   / 7

How well did you do?

1–4 marks   Try again
5–8 marks   Getting there
9–13 marks Good work
14–18 marks Excellent!

TOTAL SCORE   / 18

For more information on this topic see pages 74–75 of your Success Guide.

REPRESENTING DATA

A Choose just one answer, a, b, c, or d.

For these questions use the information shown in the frequency diagram.

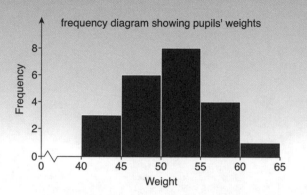

frequency diagram showing pupils' weights

1 How many pupils had a weight between 50 and 55 kg?
- a) 4
- b) 6
- c) 10
- d) 8
(1 mark)

2 How many pupils had a weight of less than 50 kg?
- a) 7
- b) 8
- c) 9
- d) 10
(1 mark)

3 How many pupils had a weight of over 60 kg?
- a) 1
- b) 2
- c) 3
- d) 4
(1 mark)

4 How many pupils took part in the survey?
- a) 8
- b) 22
- c) 5
- d) 20
(1 mark)

Score   / 4

B Answer all parts of the questions.

1 Sarah carried out a survey to find the favourite flavours of crisps of students in her class. Her results are shown in the table below.

Crisp flavour	Number of students
Cheese and Onion	7
Salt and Vinegar	10
Beef	6
Smokey Bacon	1

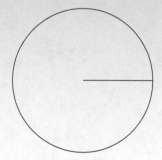

Draw an accurate pie chart to show this information.

(4 marks)

2 The number of hours of sunshine during the first seven days in May are shown on the line graph. Using the information on the graph complete the table.

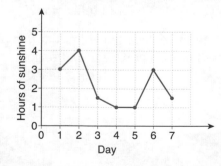

Day	1	2	3	4	5	6	7
Hrs of sunshine	3		1.5	1	1		

(3 marks)

Score   / 7

C These are GCSE style questions. Answer all parts of the questions. Show your workings (on separate paper if necessary) and include the correct units in your answers.

1 A vending machine is emptied every day. The pie chart represents the number of each type of coin in the machine.

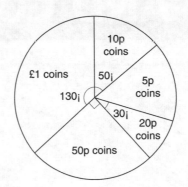

The machine contains 150 ten pence coins.

a) How many one pound coins are there?

.... (1 mark)

b) Calculate the total amount of money in the machine.

....

....

....

.... (4 marks)

2 The table shows the heights of a class of children.

Height in cm	Frequency
$130 \leq h < 135$	5
$135 \leq h < 140$	9
$140 \leq h < 145$	7
$145 \leq h < 150$	1
$150 \leq h < 155$	5
$155 \leq h < 160$	2

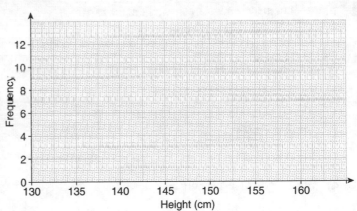

Draw a frequency polygon for this data.

(3 marks)

Score   / 8

How well did you do?

1–4 marks   Try again
5–8 marks   Getting there
9–14 marks   Good work
15–19 marks   Excellent!

TOTAL SCORE   / 19

For more information on this topic see pages 76–77 of your Success Guide.

SCATTER DIAGRAMS AND CORRELATION

A Choose just one answer, a, b, c, or d.

1 A scatter diagram is drawn to show the height and weight of some students. What type of correlation is shown?

a) zero
b) negative
c) positive
d) scattered

(1 mark)

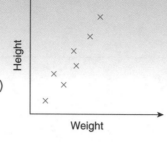

Height

Weight

2 A scatter diagram is drawn to show the maths score and the height of a group of students. What type of correlation is shown?

a) zero
b) negative
c) positive
d) scattered

(1 mark)

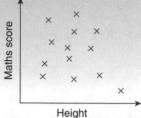

Maths score

Height

3 A scatter diagram is drawn to show the age of some cars and their value. What type of correlation would be shown?

a) zero
b) negative
c) positive
d) scattered

(1 mark)

Score   / 3

B Answer all parts of the questions.

1 Some statements have been written on card.

(Positive Correlation)   (Negative Correlation)   (No Correlation)

Decide which card best describes these relationships.

a) The temperature and the sales of ice lollies .... (1 mark)

b) The temperature and the sales of woollen gloves .... (1 mark)

c) The weight of a person and his waist measurement .... (1 mark)

d) The height of a person and his IQ .... (1 mark)

2 The scatter diagram shows the marks scored in Mathematics and Physics examinations.

a) Describe the relationship between the Mathematics and Physics scores.

.... (1 mark)

b) Draw a line of best fit on the scatter diagram. (1 mark)

c) Use your line of best fit to estimate the Mathematics score that Jonathan is likely to obtain if he has a Physics score of 75%.

.... (1 mark)

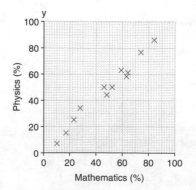

Physics (%)

Mathematics (%)

Score   / 7

C

This is a GCSE style question. Answer all parts of the question. Show all your workings (on separate paper if necessary) and include the correct units in your answers.

1 The table shows the ages of some children and the total number of hours sleep they had between noon on Saturday and noon on Sunday.

Age (years)	2	6	5	3	12	9	2	10	5	10	7	11	12	3
No. of hours sleep	15	13.1	13.2	14.8	10.1	11.8	15.6	11.6	13.5	11.8	12.8	10.2	9.5	14

a) On the scatter diagram, plot the information from the table.

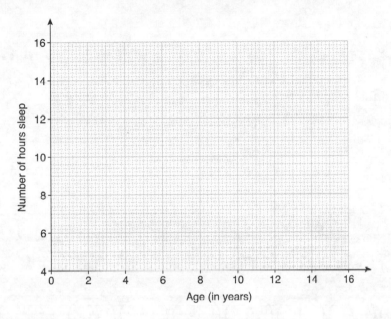

(4 marks)

b) Describe the correlation between the age of the children in years and the number of hours sleep they had.

....

.... (2 marks)

c) Draw a line of best fit on your diagram. (1 mark)

d) Estimate the total number of hours sleep for a 4-year-old child.

.... (2 marks)

e) Explain why the line of best fit only gives an estimate for the number of hours slept.

....

.... (2 marks)

Score   / 11

How well did you do?

1–5 marks   Try again
6–11 marks   Getting there
12–16 marks   Good work
17–21 marks   Excellent!

TOTAL SCORE   /21

For more information on this topic see pages 78–79 of your Success Guide.

AVERAGES 1

Choose just one answer, a, b, c, or d.

1 What is the mean of this set of data?

2 7 1 4 2 6 2 5 2 6

a) 4.2
b) 3.6
c) 3.7
d) 3.9   (1 mark)

2 What is the median value of the set of data used in question 1?

a) 2   b) 3
c) 4   d) 5   (1 mark)

3 What is the range of this set of data?

2, 7, 1, 4, 11, 9, 6

a) 1
b) 6
c) 11
d) 10   (1 mark)

4 A die is thrown and the scores are noted. The results are shown in the table below. What is the mean die score?

Die score	1	2	3	4	5	6
Frequency	12	15	10	8	14	13

a) 5   b) 3
c) 4   d) 3.5   (1 mark)

5 Using the information in the table above, what is the modal score?

a) 15
b) 2
c) 4
d) 8   (1 mark)

Score   / 5

Answer all parts of the questions.

1 Here are some number cards.

(8) (7) (11) (4) (2) (1) (3) (12) (4) (4)

Decide whether the following statements, which refer to the number cards above, are true or false.

a) The range of the number cards is 1–11 .... (1 mark)

b) The mean of the number cards is 5.6 .... (1 mark)

c) The median of the number cards is 5 .... (1 mark)

d) The mode of the number cards is 4 .... (1 mark)

2 A baked beans factory claims that 'on average, a tin of baked beans contains 142 beans'.

In order to check the accuracy of this claim, a sample of 20 tins were taken and the number of beans in each tin counted.

Number of beans	137	138	139	140	141	142	143	144
Number of tins	1	1	1	2	5	4	4	2

a) Calculate the mean number of beans per tin. .... (1 mark)

b) Explain briefly whether you think the manufacturer is justified in making its claim.

.... (1 mark)

3 The mean of 7, 9 10, 18, x and 17 is 13. What is the value of x? .... (2 marks)

Score   / 8

78

C These are GCSE style questions. Answer all parts of the questions. Show your workings (on separate paper if necessary) and include the correct units in your answers.

1 Some students took a test. The table gives information about their marks in the test.

Mark	Frequency
3	2
4	5
5	11
6	2

Work out the mean mark.

....

.... (3 marks)

2 Simon has sat three examinations. His mean score is 65. To pass the unit, he needs to get an average of 69. What score must he get in the final examination to pass the unit?

....

.... (3 marks)

3 A company employs 3 women and 7 men.

The mean weekly wage of the 10 employees is £464.

The mean weekly wage of the 3 women is £520.

Caloulato tho moan wookly wago of tho 7 mon.

....

.... (4 marks)

4 Find the three-point moving average for the following data:

   2   5   3   6   2   1   4

....

....

.... (5 marks)

Score   / 15

How well did you do?

1–6 marks   Try again
7–12 marks   Getting there
13–21 marks   Good work
22–28 marks   Excellent!

TOTAL SCORE   / 28

For more information on this topic see pages 80–81 of your Success Guide.

AVERAGES 2

A Choose just one answer, a, b, c, or d.

The following questions are based on the information given in the table below about the time taken in seconds to swim 50 metres.

Time (seconds)	Frequency (f)
$0 \leq t < 30$	1
$30 \leq t < 60$	2
$60 \leq t < 90$	4
$90 \leq t < 120$	6
$120 \leq t < 150$	7
$150 \leq t < 180$	2

1 How many people swam 50 metres in less than 60 seconds?

a) 2   b) 4
c) 3   d) 6   (1 mark)

2 Which of the intervals is the modal class?
a) $60 \leq t < 90$ b) $120 \leq t < 150$
c) $30 \leq t < 60$ d) $90 \leq t < 120$
(1 mark)

3 Which of the class intervals contains the median value?
a) $90 \leq t < 120$ b) $150 \leq t < 180$
c) $120 \leq t < 150$ d) $60 \leq t < 90$
(1 mark)

4 What is the estimate for the mean time to swim 50 metres?
a) 105 seconds   b) 385 seconds
c) 100 seconds   d) 125 seconds
(1 mark)

Score   / 4

B Answer all parts of the questions.

1 The length of some seedlings are shown in the table below.

Length in mm	Number of seedlings
$0 \leq L < 10$	3
$10 \leq L < 20$	5
$20 \leq L < 30$	9
$30 \leq L < 40$	2
$40 \leq L < 50$	1

Calculate an estimate for the mean length of the seedlings.

Mean = ... (4 marks)

2 The stem and leaf diagram shows the marks gained by some students in a Mathematics examination.

Stem	Leaf
1	2 5 7
2	6 9
3	4 5 5 7
4	2 7 7 7 7
5	2

Using the stem and leaf diagram, calculate these.

a) the mode   .... (1 mark)

b) the median   .... (1 mark)

c) the range   .... (1 mark)

Stem = 10 marks

Key: 1|2 = 12 marks

Score   / 7

C These are GCSE style questions. Answer all parts of the questions. Show your workings (on separate paper if necessary) and include the correct units in your answers.

1 A psychologist records the time, to the nearest minute, taken by 20 students to complete a logic problem.

Here are the results.

12	22	31	36	35	14	27	23	19	25
15	17	15	27	32	38	41	18	27	18

Draw a stem and leaf diagram to show this information.

(4 marks)

2 John asks 100 people how much they spent last year on newspapers. The results are in the table below.

Amount £ (x)	frequency
$0 \leq x < 10$	12
$10 \leq x < 20$	20
$20 \leq x < 30$	15
$30 \leq x < 40$	18
$40 \leq x < 50$	14
$50 \leq x < 60$	18
$60 \leq x < 70$	3

a) Calculate an estimate of the mean amount spent on newspapers.

.... (4 marks)

b) Explain briefly why this value of the mean is only an estimate.

.... (1 mark)

c) Calculate the class interval in which the median lies.

.... (2 marks)

Score   / 11

How well did you do?

1–6 marks   Try again
7–11 marks   Getting there
12–16 marks   Good work
17–22 marks   Excellent!

TOTAL SCORE / 22

For more information on this topic see pages 82–83 of your Success Guide.

CUMULATIVE FREQUENCY GRAPHS

A

Choose just one answer, a, b, c, or d.

The data below shows the number of letters delivered to each of the 15 houses in Whelan Avenue (arranged in order of size).

0, 0, 1, 1, 1, 1, 1, 1, 2, 2, 2, 3, 4, 5, 5

Use the information above to answer these questions.

1 What is the median number of letters delivered?

a) 0
b) 2
c) 1
d) 5   (1 mark)

2 What is the lower quartile for the number of letters delivered?

a) 0   b) 2
c) 3   d) 1   (1 mark)

3 What is the upper quartile for the number of letters delivered?

a) 0   b) 2
c) 3   d) 1   (1 mark)

4 What is the interquartile range for the number of letters delivered?

a) 2   b) 3
c) 4   d) 5   (1 mark)

Score   / 4

B

Answer all parts of the questions.

1 The table shows the examination marks of some Year 10 pupils in their end of year Maths examination.

Examination mark	Frequency	Cumulative frequency
0–10	4	
11–20	6	
21–30	11	
31–40	24	
41–50	18	
51–60	7	
61–70	3	

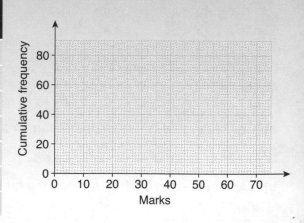

a) Complete the cumulative frequency column in the table above.   (2 marks)

b) Draw the cumulative frequency graph.   (3 marks)

c) From your graph, find the median mark. .... (1 mark)

d) From your graph, find the interquartile range. .... (2 marks)

e) If 16 pupils were given a grade A in the examination, what is the minimum score needed for a grade A?

.... (2 marks)

Score   / 10

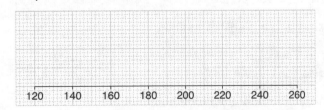

C These are GCSE style questions. Answer all parts of the questions. Show your workings (on separate paper if necessary) and include the correct units in your answers.

1 The table gives information about the time, to the nearest minute, taken to run a marathon.

Time (nearest minute)	Frequency	Cumulative frequency
$120 < t \le 140$	1	
$140 < t \le 160$	8	
$160 < t \le 180$	24	
$180 < t \le 200$	29	
$200 < t \le 220$	10	
$220 < t \le 240$	5	
$240 < t \le 260$	3	

a) Complete the table to show the cumulative frequency for this data. (2 marks)

b) Draw the cumulative frequency graph for the data.

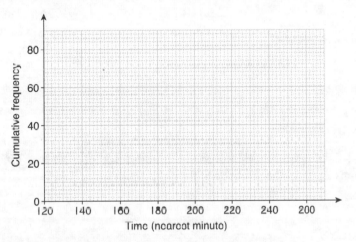

(3 marks)

c) Use your graph to work out an estimate for these.

   i) The interquartile range .... minutes (2 marks)

   ii) The number of runners with a time of more than 205 minutes

       .... runners (1 mark)

d) Draw a box plot for this data.

(3 marks)

Score   /11

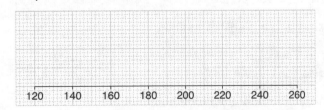
TOTAL SCORE   /25

For more information on this topic see pages 84–85 of your Success Guide.

PROBABILITY 1

Choose just one answer, a, b, c, or d.

1 A bag of sweets contains 5 hard centres and 3 soft centres. What is the probability of choosing a hard centre if the sweet is drawn out of the bag at random?
a) $\frac{3}{5}$　　　b) $\frac{3}{8}$
c) $\frac{5}{8}$　　　d) $\frac{1}{2}$　　(1 mark)

2 The probability that Highbury football club win a football match is $\frac{12}{17}$. What is the probability that they do not win the football match?
a) $\frac{5}{12}$　　　　b) $\frac{17}{29}$
c) $\frac{12}{17}$　　　　d) $\frac{5}{17}$　　(1 mark)

3 A fair die is thrown 600 times. On how many of these throws would you expect to get a 4?
a) 40　　　　b) 600
c) 100　　　d) 580　　(1 mark)

4 A fair die is thrown 500 times. If a 6 comes up 87 times, what is the relative frequency?
a) $\frac{1}{6}$
b) $\frac{87}{500}$
c) $\frac{10}{600}$
d) $\frac{1}{587}$　　(1 mark)

5 The probability that it will rain tomorrow is 0.35. What is the probability that it will not rain tomorrow?
a) 0.65
b) 0.35
c) 0.25
d) 1.35　　(1 mark)

Score ___ / 5

B **Answer all parts of the questions.**

1 The letters M A T H E M A T I C S are each placed on a separate piece of card and put into a bag. Stuart picks out a card at random. What is the probability he picks these?

a) The letter T　　.................................

b) The letter M　　.................................

c) The letters A or C　.................................

d) The letter R　　.................................　　(4 marks)

2 The probability that Robert wins a tennis match is 0.35. What is the probability that Robert does not win the tennis match?　.................　(1 mark)

3 Decide whether each of these statements is true or false.

a) The probability of getting a six when a fair die is thrown is $\frac{1}{6}$　.................　(1 mark)

b) The probability of passing a test in Physics is 0.3. If 100 students sit the test, the number expected to pass would be 3.　.................　(1 mark)

c) The probability that Conkers football team win a match is 0.8. The probability that they will not win the game is 0.4.　.................　(1 mark)

4 The probability of achieving a grade A in French is 0.2. If 500 students sit the exam, how many would you expect to achieve a grade A?　.................　(2 marks)

Score ___ / 10

84

C These are GCSE style questions. Answer all parts of the questions. Show your workings (on separate paper if necessary) and include the correct units in your answers.

1 There are 20 different coloured sweets in a jar. The colour of each sweet can be red, green, yellow or blue. The table shows how many sweets of each colour are in the jar.

Colour	Red	Green	Yellow	Blue
Probability	4	5	7	4

Reece picks one sweet at random from the jar.

a) Write down the probability that he will pick these.

   i) A green sweet .... (1 mark)

   ii) A yellow sweet .... (1 mark)

b) Write down the probability that he will get a blue sweet. .... (2 marks)

2 A youth club has 75 members. The table shows some information about the members.

	Under 13 years old	13 years and over	Total
Boys	15		42
Girls		21	
Total			75

a) Complete the table. (3 marks)

b) One of these members is picked at random.

   Write down the probability that the member is under 13 years old .... (1 mark)

3 A bag contains different coloured beads.

The probability of taking a bead of a particular colour at random is as follows.

Colour	Red	White	Blue	Pink
Probability	0.25	0.1		0.3

Jackie is going to take a bead at random and then put it back in the bag.

a) i) Work out the probability that Jackie will take out a blue bead. .... (2 marks)

   ii) Write down the probability that Jackie will take out a black bead. .... (1 mark)

b) Jackie will take out a bead from the bag at random 200 times, replacing the bead each time. Work out an estimate for the number of times that Jackie takes a red bead.

.... (2 marks)

Score   / 13

How well did you do?

1–6 marks	Try again
7–13 marks	Getting there
14–21 marks	Good work
22–28 marks	Excellent!

TOTAL SCORE   / 28

For more information on this topic see pages 86–87 of your Success Guide.

PROBABILITY 2

Choose just one answer, a, b, c or d.

1 Two dice are thrown and their scores are added. What is the probability of a score of 5?

a) $\frac{1}{2}$

b) $\frac{2}{12}$

c) $\frac{4}{36}$

d) $\frac{5}{36}$ (1 mark)

2 Two dice are thrown and their scores are multiplied. What is the probability of a score of 1?

a) $\frac{1}{36}$

b) $\frac{1}{12}$

c) $\frac{2}{12}$

d) $\frac{2}{36}$ (1 mark)

3 The probability that it snows on Christmas day is 0.2. What is the probability that it will snow on Christmas day in two consecutive years?

a) 0.04   b) 0.4

c) 0.2   d) 0.16 (1 mark)

4 The probability that Fiona is in the hockey team is 0.7. The probability that she is picked for the netball team is 0.3. What is the probability that she is picked for both teams?

a) 1.0   b) 0.1

c) 0.12   d) 0.21 (1 mark)

Score   / 4

B **Answer all parts of the questions.**

1 Two spinners are spun at the same time and their scores are added.

Spinner 1

3	3
2	1

Spinner 2

6	2
3	1

a) Complete the sample space diagram to show the outcomes.

Spinner 1

Spinner 2	1	2	3	3
1	2			
2			5	
3		5		
6		8	9	

(2 marks)

b) Find the probability of these.

i) A score of 4 .... (1 mark)

ii) A score of 9 .... (1 mark)

iii) A score of 1 .... (1 mark)

2 The probability that Michelle finishes first in a swimming race is 0.3. Michelle swims two races. Work out the probability that Michelle wins both races. .... (2 marks)

3 There are 13 counters in a bag: 7 are red and the rest are white. A counter is picked at random, its colour noted and then it is replaced. A second counter is then chosen. What is the probability of choosing these?

a) Two red counters .... (2 marks)

b) A red and a white counter .... (3 marks)

Score   / 12

C These are GCSE style questions. Answer all parts of the questions. Show your workings (on separate paper if necessary) and include the correct units in your answers.

1 Two fair dice are thrown together and their scores are added.

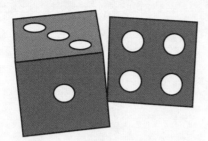

a) Work out the probability of a score of 7. .... (2 marks)

b) Work out the probability of a score of 9. .... (2 marks)

2 Kevin and Nathan challenge each other to a game of Monopoly and a game of pool. A draw is not possible in either game.

The probability that Kevin wins at Monopoly is 0.4.

The probability that Nathan wins at pool is 0.7.

a) The probability tree diagram has been started in the space provided.

Label clearly the branches of the probability tree diagram.

Complete the tree diagram.

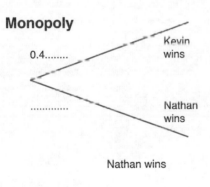
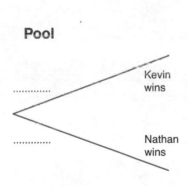

(3 marks)

b) What is the probability that Nathan wins both games? .... (2 marks)

Score   / 9

How well did you do?

1–6 marks   Try again
7–12 marks   Getting there
13–19 marks   Good work
20–25 marks   Excellent!

TOTAL SCORE   / 25

For more information on this topic see pages 88–89 of your Success Guide.

MIXED GCSE-STYLE QUESTIONS

Answer these questions. Show full working out.

1 Here is a diagram showing the side views of a model.

The cubes are either purple or white.

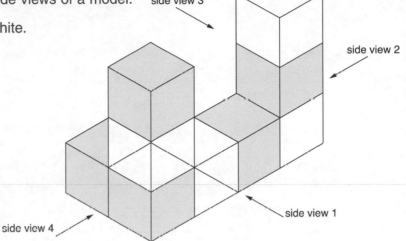

side view 3

side view 2

side view 1

side view 4

These drawings show the side views of the model. Write the numbers to show which side view each drawing represents.

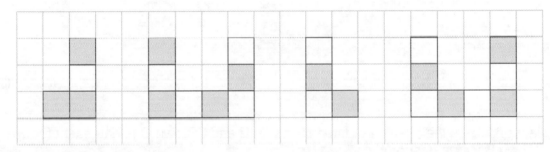

a) side view .... **b)** side view .... **c)** side view .... **d)** side view ....

(2 marks)

2 Work these out.

a) 4.23 × 6.1 .... (2 marks)

b) 10.53 ÷ 3.9 .... (2 marks)

c) Estimate the value of $\dfrac{8.9 \times 5.2}{10.1}$ .... (2 marks)

3 The cost of 8 pencils is £1.92.

a) Work out the cost of 14 pencils.

£ ....

(2 marks)

b) The probability that the lead will break on the first go is 0.12. Work out the probability that a pencil picked at random will not break.

.... (1 mark)

4 Here are the first four terms of an arithmetic sequence.

5, 9, 13, 17

Find an expression, in terms of *n*, for the *n*th term of the sequence.

....

(2 marks)

5 Draw the graph of $y = 4 - 3x$ on the grid below.

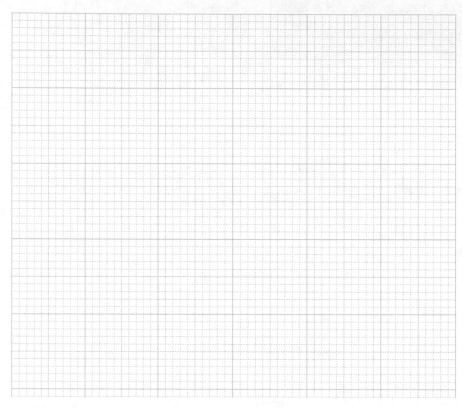

(3 marks)

6 The diagram shows the position of three towns: A, B and C. Town C is due east of towns A and B. Town B is due east of A.

A   B   C

Town B is $3\frac{1}{3}$ miles from town A

Town C is $1\frac{1}{4}$ miles from town B.

Calculate the number of miles between town A and town C.

.... miles

(3 marks)

7 Here are the ages in years of the members of a golf club.

9	42	37	28	36	44	47	43	62	19	17	36	40
56	58	32	18	41	52	42	54	38	27	29	32	51

In the space provided draw a stem and leaf diagram to show these ages. (3 marks)

8 The diagram shows a shape, made from a semicircle, a rectangle and a triangle.

The diameter of the semicircle is 4 cm.

The length of the rectangle is 7 cm.

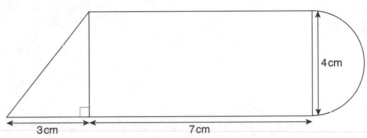

Calculate the perimeter of the shape.

Give your answer correct to 3 significant figures.

.... cm (5 marks)

9 $2.4 \times 320 = 768$

Use this result to write down the answer to these.

a) 2.4×32 .... (1 mark)

b) 2.4×3.2 .... (1 mark)

c) 0.24×0.32 .... (1 mark)

10

a) Solve $5x - 2 = 3(x + 6)$ $x =$ .... (2 marks)

b) Solve $\dfrac{3 - 2x}{4} = 2$

$x =$ .... (2 marks)

c) i) Factorise $x^2 - 10x + 24$. .... (2 marks)

ii) Hence solve $x^2 - 10x + 24$ .... (1 mark)

d) Simplify $\dfrac{x^2 + 2^2}{x^2 + 5^2 + 6}$ .... (3 marks)

e) Simplify these.

i) $p^4 \times p^6$ .... (1 mark)

ii) $\dfrac{p^7}{p^3}$ .... (1 mark)

iii) $\dfrac{p^4 \times p^5}{p}$ .... (1 mark)

11 The times, in minutes, to finish an assault course, are listed in order.

8, 12, 12, 13, 15, 17, 22, 23, 23, 27, 29

a) Find these.

i) The lower quartile   ....

ii) The interquartile range   ....   (2 marks)

b) Draw a box plot for this data.   (3 marks)

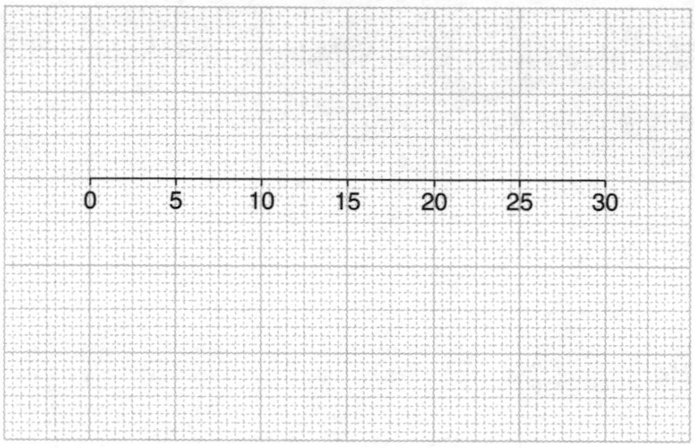

12 A rectangular field has the dimensions shown in the diagram.

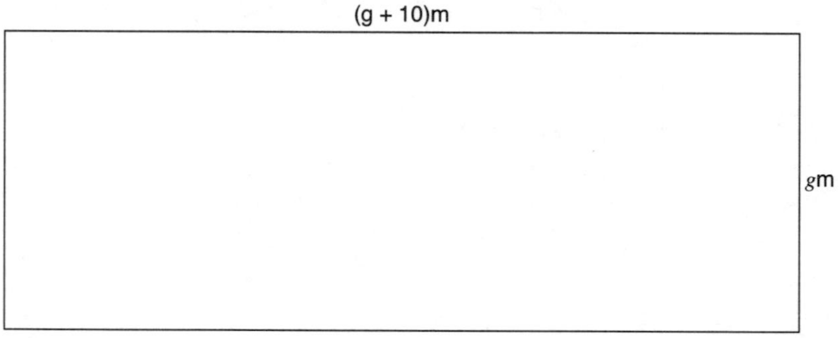

$(g + 10)$m

gm

a) Write down an expression, in terms of g, for the area in m^2 of the field.

....   (2 marks)

b) Given that the area of the field is 11 m^2, show that $g^2 + 10g = 11$

....

....   (3 marks)

c) Solve the quadratic equation and find the length and width of the field.

Length ....

Width ....   (3 marks)

13 a) Megan bought a TV for £700.

Each year, the TV depreciated by 20%.

Work out the value of the TV two years after she bought it.

....   (3 marks)

b) In a '20% off' sale, William bought a DVD player for £300. What was the original price of the DVD player before the sale?

£ ....

(3 marks)

14 The diagram shows a right-angled triangle.

PQ = 14.2 cm

Angle PRQ = 90°

Angle RPQ = 38°

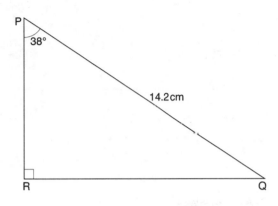

Find the length of the side QR. Give your answer to 3 significant figures.

.................................cm

(3 marks)

15 The table gives the times to the nearest minute to complete a puzzle.

Time (nearest min)	Frequency
$0 \leq t < 10$	5
$10 \leq t < 20$	12
$20 \leq t < 30$	8
$30 \leq t < 40$	5

Calculate an estimate for the mean number of minutes to complete the puzzle.

Mean ....minutes

(4 marks)

16

$b = \dfrac{a + c}{ac}$

$a = 3.2 \times 10^5$

$c = 5 \times 10^6$

Calculate the value of b.

Give your answer in standard form.

....

(2 marks)

17

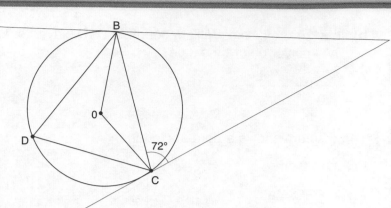

D, B and C are points on a circle with centre O.

AB and AC are tangents to the circle.

Angle ACB = 72°.

a) Explain why angle OCB is 18°.

....

.... (1 mark)

b) Calculate the size of angle BDC.

....

Give reasons for your answer.

.... (3 marks)

18 The diagram shows the graphs of these equations: $x + y = 4$, $y = x - 2$

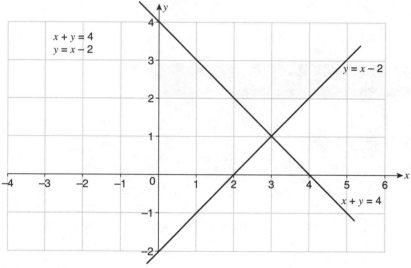

a) Use the diagram to solve these simultaneous equations.

$x + y = 4$ $x =$ ....

$y + 2 = x$ $y =$ .... (4 marks)

b) On the grid, shade the region satisfied by these inequalities.

$x + y \leq 4$, $y \geq x - 2$ (2 marks)

How well did you do?

1–23 marks   Try again
24–37 marks   Getting there
38–59 marks   Good work
60–78 marks   Excellent!

TOTAL SCORE   / 78

Answers to mixed questions

1 **a)** side view 4

   b) side view 1

   c) side view 2

   d) side view 3

2 **a)** 25.803

   b) 2.7

   c) 4.5

3 **a)** £3.36

   b) 0.88

4 $4n + 1$

5

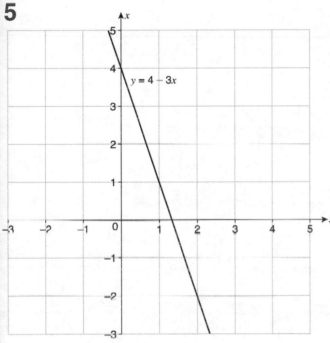

$y = 4 - 3x$

6 $4\frac{7}{12}$ miles

7

```
0    9
1    7 8 9
2    7 8 9
3    2 2 6 6 7 8
4    0 1 2 2 3 4 7
5    1 2 4 6 8
6    2
```

1|7 means 17 years

stem = 10 years

8 Perimeter is 25.3 cm.

9 **a)** 76.8

   b) 7.68

   c) 0.0768

10 **a)** $x = 10$

   b) $x = -2.5$

   c) i) $(x - 4)(x - 6)$

      ii) $x = 4$ and $x = 6$

   d) $\dfrac{x(x + 2)}{(x + 2)(x + 3)} = \dfrac{x}{(x + 3)}$

   e) i) p^{10}

      ii) p^4

      iii) p^8

11 **a)** i) lower quartile = 12

      ii) interquartile range = 11

   b)

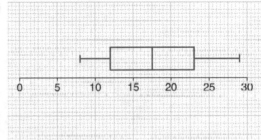

12 **a)** $g(g + 10) = g^2 + 10g$

   b) $g^2 + 10g = 11$ since area = 11 cm^2

   c) $g^2 + 10g - 11 = 0$

      $(g + 11)(g - 1) = 0$

      $g = -11$ or $g = 1$

      Length = 11 cm

      Width = 1 cm

13 **a)** £448

   b) £375

14 QR = 8.74 cm

15 19.3 minutes

16 3.325×10^{-6}

17 a) The radius and tangent meet at 90°.
Since angle ACB = 72° then angle
OCB = 90° − 72° = 18°.

b) Angle OCB = angle OBC = 18°

Angle BOC = 180° − (2 × 18°) = 144°

Angle BDC = 144° ÷ 2, since the angle
subtended at the circle is twice the
angle at the circumference.

Angle BDC = 72°

18 a)

$x = 3$

$y = 1$

b)

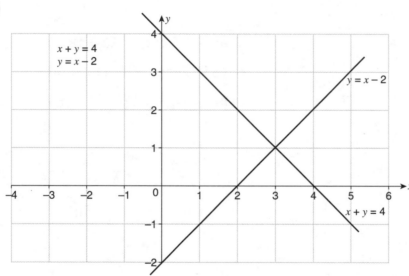

Letts

GCSE

SUCCESS

VISUAL REVISION GUIDE

QUESTIONS & ANSWERS

BRAND NEW

INTERMEDIATE GCSE MATHS

Fiona C Mapp

ANSWER BOOK

NUMBER

TYPES OF NUMBERS

A
1. d
2. a
3. d
4. c
5. a

B
1. a) true
   b) false
   c) true
   d) false
2. a) 2
   b) 10
   c) 64
   d) 3
   e) −5
   f) 81
3. $72 = 2^3 \times 3^2$
4. $a = 2, b = 2$
5. 60
6. 8
7. true

C
1. a) 1, 9, 16, 25
   b) 1, 6, 12, 24
   c) 11, 17
   d) 9
2. a) i) $56 = 2 \times 2 \times 2 \times 7$
      ii) $60 = 2 \times 2 \times 3 \times 5$
   b) HCF = 4
   c) LCM = 840
3. $360 = 2^3 \times 3^2 \times 5$
   Hence $a = 3, b = 2, c = 1$

POSITIVE AND NEGATIVE NUMBERS

A
1. b
2. c
3. a
4. d
5. b

B
1. a) −7 and 5
   b) −7 and −3
   c) 5 and −3
2. -3×4 → 10
   $12 \div (-2)$ → −1
   $-4 - (-3)$ → −12
   $-5 \times (-2)$ → 4
   $-20 \div (-5)$ → −6
3. a) 10
   b) −10
   c) 14
4.

		−16		
	−5		−11	
	3	−8	−3	
5	−2	−6	3	

C
1. a) 18° C
   b) i) 17° C
      ii) 19° C
2. a) 12° C
   b) 4°C
   c) −11° C

FRACTIONS

A
1. c
2. a
3. b
4. c
5. a

B
1. a) $\frac{4}{22}$ b) $\frac{28}{49}$
   c) $\frac{1}{4}$ d) $\frac{36}{51}$
2. a) $2\frac{1}{2}$ b) $1\frac{2}{3}$
   c) $4\frac{1}{2}$ d) $1\frac{1}{11}$
3. a) $\frac{5}{9}$ b) $\frac{17}{44}$
   c) $\frac{3}{14}$ d) 3
   e) $\frac{2}{3}$ f) $\frac{5}{9}$
   g) $\frac{7}{8}$ h) $2\frac{34}{49}$
4. a) $\frac{1}{7}$ $\frac{3}{10}$ $\frac{1}{2}$ $\frac{2}{3}$ $\frac{1}{4}$ $\frac{4}{5}$
   b) $\frac{1}{9}$ $\frac{2}{7}$ $\frac{1}{3}$ $\frac{2}{5}$ $\frac{5}{8}$ $\frac{3}{4}$
5. a) true
   b) false

C
1. Jonathan, since $\frac{2}{3}$ is greater than $\frac{3}{5}$.
2. a) $1\frac{7}{15}$ b) $\frac{16}{33}$
   c) $\frac{8}{63}$ d) $\frac{3}{4}$
3. $\frac{7}{15}$
4. 28 students

DECIMALS

A
1. c
2. c
3. b
4. d
5. b

B
1. a) false b) true
   c) true d) true
   e) true
2. 7.09, 7.102, 7.32, 7.321, 8.31, 8.315
3. a) Molly
   b) 1.201 seconds
   c) 0.002 seconds
4. a) 16 b) 100
   c) 2 000 d) 0.1
   e) 24 f) 0.001

C
1. a) 6.14, 6.141, 7.208, 7.29, 7.42
   b) 1.28
   c) 34.199
   d) i) 7.21
      ii) 6.14
2. a) 0.01
   b) 0.1
   c) 0.001

PERCENTAGES 1

A
1. c
2. c
3. a
4. d
5. b

B
1. 10% of 30 → 16
   40% of 40 → 5
   5% of 15 → 3
   25% of 20 → 0.75
2. £26 265
3. 39%
4. 77%
5. £20
6. 40%

C
1. a) £30.63
   b) £339.15
2. 20%
3. £70

PERCENTAGES 2

A
1. d
2. a
3. c
4. b

B
1. £168.03
2. £75.60
3. £6 969.60
4. £515.88
5. £135 475.20
6. 80.2 pence

C
1. a) £1 000
   b) £160
2. £1 337.11
3. a) 3.5%
   b) £757.12

FRACTIONS, DECIMALS AND PERCENTAGES

A
1. c
2. b
3. d
4. d
5. a

B
1.

Fraction	Decimal	Percentage
$\frac{2}{5}$	0.4	40%
$\frac{1}{20}$	0.05	5%
$\frac{1}{3}$	0.3	33.3%
$\frac{1}{25}$	0.04	4%
$\frac{1}{4}$	0.25	25%
$\frac{1}{8}$	0.125	12.5%

2. 30%, $\frac{1}{3}$, 0.37, $\frac{3}{8}$, $\frac{1}{2}$, 0.62, 92%
3. 'Rosebushes' is cheaper because $\frac{1}{4}$ = 25% which is greater than the offer at 'Gardens are Us'.

C
1. $\frac{1}{8}$, 25%, 0.27, $\frac{1}{3}$, $\frac{2}{5}$, 0.571, 72%
2. a) Ed's Electricals: £225
      Sheila's Bargains: £217.38
      Gita's TV shop: £232
      Maximum price = £232
      Minimum price = £217.38
   b) £200
3. Both will give the same answer because increasing by 20% is the same as multiplying by 1.2. Finding 10% then doubling it gives 20%, which when you add it to 40, is the same as increasing £40 by 20%.

APPROXIMATIONS AND USING A CALCULATOR

A
1. b
2. d
3. c
4. c
5. d

B
1. a) true
   b) false
   c) false
   d) true
2. a) 100
   b) 90

3. a) 365 (3 s.f.)
   b) 10.2 (3 s.f.)
   c) 6 320 (3 s.f.)

C
1. a) 30 and 80
   b) 2 400
   c) 49
2. 7.09 (3s.f.)
3. a) 5.9371025
   b) $\frac{30 \times 6}{40 - 10} = \frac{180}{30} = 6$
4. $\frac{1}{4}$
5. a) − 856.85965
   b) − 857

RATIO

A
1. c
2. d
3. c
4. d
5. b

B
1. a) 1 : 1.5
   b) 1 : 1.6̇
   c) 1 : 3
2. 1 200 ml
3. a) £10.25
   b) 48 g
4. £25 000
5. 4.5 days

C
1. Vicky £6 400
   Tracy £8 000
2. butter 125 g
   sugar 100 g
   eggs 5
   flour 112.5 g
   milk 37.5 ml
3. 6 days

INDICES

A
1. a
2. c
3. d
4. a
5. b

B
1. a) 64
   b) 32
   c) 81
2. a) false
   b) false
   c) true
   d) true
   e) false
   f) true
3. a) $6a^2$
   b) $3m^2$
   c) $20a^3b^5$
   d) 1
   e) $16a^8$
   f) $\frac{3}{4}a^{-3}$
   g) a^{20}
   h) $27a^6b^9$
4. a) n = 6
   b) n = 10
   c) n = 9
5. a) $4x^{-2}$
   b) a^2b^{-3}
   c) $3y^{-5}$

C
1. a) p^7
   b) n^{-4} or $\frac{1}{n^4}$
   c) a^6
   d) $4ab$

2 a) 1
  b) $\frac{1}{25}$
  c) 648
3 a) i) 1
    ii) $\frac{1}{16}$
    iii) ± 4
  b) 5^4
4 a) $6a^5$
  b) $3a$
  c) $\dfrac{1}{4b^2}$
5 a) i) 1
    ii) ± 5
    iii) $\frac{1}{8}$
  b) 3^{-10} or $\dfrac{1}{3^{10}}$

STANDARD INDEX FORM

A
1 b
2 b
3 a
4 b
5 b

B
1 a) 2.71×10^3
  b) 4.27×10^6
  c) 2.71×10^{-2}
  d) 3.6×10^{-3}
  e) 4×10^6
  f) 4.1×10^{-4}
2 a) true
  b) false
  c) false
  d) false
3 a) 8×10^7
  b) 1.4×10^4
  c) 3×10^{16}
  d) 8×10^3

C
1 a) i) 207 000
    ii) 4.6×10^{-5}
  b) 3.5×10^{12}
2 2.2×10^{12}
3 2.6×10^{-6}
4 a) 8.19×10^3
  b) 7.56×10^3
  c) 6×10^4
  d) 2.225×10^8
5 1.0×10^{-7} grams

ALGEBRA

ALGEBRA 1

A
1 b
2 c
3 d
4 d
5 c

B
1 a) true
  b) true
  c) false
2 $T = 6b + 0.67m$
3 a) 4
  b) 5
  c) 8

C
1 a) $6n$
  b) $6ab$
2 a) $p = 5n - 6$
  b) $p = -16$
3 $V = 8.9$ (2 s.f.)
4 She has forgotten to square root 37 to find v.

ALGEBRA 2

A
1 a
2 c
3 d
4 a
5 c

B
1 a) $3n - 9$
  b) $5(n + 3)$
  c) $n^2 - 3n + 2$
  d) $8(n + 2)$
2 a) $5(2n + 3)$
  b) $12(2 - 3n)$
  c) $(n + 1)(n + 5)$
  d) $(n - 8)(n + 8)$
  e) $(n + 1)(n - 4)$
3 a) $b = \dfrac{p + 4}{3}$
  b) $b = \pm\sqrt{(4y + 6)}$
  c) $b = \dfrac{2 - 5n}{3}$

C
1 a) $4x + 7$
  b) i) $6(a + 2)$
    ii) $5a(2a - 3b)$
  c) i) $(n + 2)(n + 3)$
    ii) $2/(n + 2)$
  d) $(n + m)(n + m - 2)$
2 a) $y = \pm(sr)(4p - 3)$
  b) $y = 2p + 2$
3 $(n - 1)2 + n + (n - 1)$
  $n^2 - 2n + 1 + n + n - 1$
  $= n^2 - 2n + 1 + 2n - 1$
  $= n^2$
4 a) $5a$
  b) i) $3(n - 4)$
    ii) $4pq(2p - 3q)$
  c) i) $(a - 1)(a + 5)$
    ii) $a = +1$
       $a = -5$

EQUATIONS 1

A
1 c
2 a
3 d
4 b
5 c

D
1 a) $n = 5$
  b) $n = 36$
  c) $n = 7$
  d) $n = 5.5$
  e) $n = 25$
  f) $n = 4$
2 a) $n = 3$
  b) $n = 5$
  c) $n = 4$
  d) $n = 14$
3 a) $n = 0, n = 4$
  b) $n = -5, n = -1$
  c) $n = 3, n = 2$
  d) $n = -4, n = 7$
4 $2n + (n + 30) + (n - 10) = 180$
  $4n + 20 = 180$
  $n = 40°$

C
1 a) $m = 3$
  b) $p = \frac{6}{10}$ or $p = \frac{3}{5}$
  c) $x = 6$
  d) $\dfrac{3w + 2(3w + 2)}{6} = \dfrac{1}{3}$
     $3w + 6w + 4 = \dfrac{6}{3}$
     $9w + 4 = 2$
     $9w = -2$
     $w = -\dfrac{2}{9}$
2 a) $(x - 1)(x - 3)$
  b) $x = 1$ and $x = 3$
3 a) $9x + 4$
  b) $x = 2$
     Shortest side = 3 cm

EQUATIONS AND INEQUALITIES

A
1 a
2 d
3 c
4 d
5 c

B
1 a) $a = 2$ b) $a = 3$
     $b = 4$ $b = 9$
  c) $a = 9$ d) $a = 3$
     $b = -2$ $b = -2$
2 5.6, -3.6
3 a) $x < 2$
  b) $x \geq 6$
  c) $1 \leq x \leq 4$
  d) $\frac{1}{3} < x \leq 2$

C
1 a) $-3, -2, -1, 0, 1, 2$
  b) $P \leq 2$
2 $x = 2.7$
3 $x = -3$
  $y = 1.5$
4 a) $a = 1$ b) $a - 3$
     $b = 2$ $b = 2$

NUMBER PATTERNS AND SEQUENCES

A
1 d
2 a
3 c
4 b

B
1 a) 10, 12
  b) 16, 19
  c) 25, 36
  d 0.75, 0.375
2 a) Fibonacci
  b) powers of 10
  c) cube numbers
3 a) 22
  b) $3n + 4$
4 a) false
  b) false
  c) true

C
1 a) $2, 1, \frac{1}{6}$
  b) $5n - 3$
2 $20n + 11$
3 $4n - 1$
4 $10 - 2n$

STRAIGHT LINE GRAPHS

A
1 b
2 d
3 b
4 c
5 a

B
1 a)

x	-2	-1	0	1	2
y	8	7	6	5	4

  b) i)

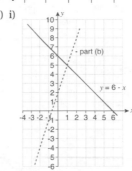

ii) $y = 3x + 2$
  c) (1, 5)
2 $y = 3 - 2x$ and $y = 4 - 2x$

C
1 a) Gradient = $-\frac{2}{3}$
  b) $3y + 2x = 6$ or $y = -\frac{2}{3}x + 2$
  c)

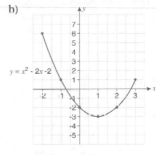

  d) (3, 2)

CURVED GRAPHS

A
1 b
2 d
3 c
4 d
5 b

B
1 a)

x	-2	-1	0	1	2	3
y	6	1	-2	-3	-2	1

  b)

$y = x^2 - 2x - 2$

  c) i) $y = -3$
    ii) $x = 2.7, x = -0.62$

C
1 a)

x	-2	-1	0	1	2	3
	-12	-5	-4	-3	4	23

  b)

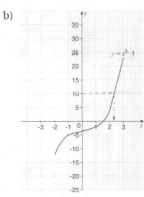

$y = x^3 - 1$

  c) i) $x = 1.55$
    ii) $x = 2.3$

INTERPRETING GRAPHS

A
1 c
2 d
3 a
4 d

B
1 Vase A matches graph ii
  Vase B matches graph i
  Vase C matches graph iii

2 Statement 1 with graph C
  Statement 2 with graph B
  Statement 3 with graph A

C

1 a) He may have decided to have a rest, met somebody and stopped to talk, had a flat tyre.
  (Any reasonable explanation, which implies that he stopped.)

  b) 13.3 Km/h

  c)

  d) approximately 1415

SHAPE, SPACE AND MEASURES

SYMMETRY AND CONSTRUCTIONS

A
1 b
2 a
3 a
4 c
5 b

B
1 a)
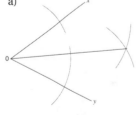

  b)
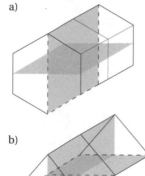

2 a)
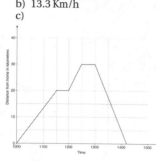

  b) 50°

3
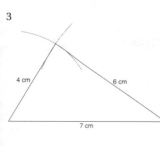

C
1 a)
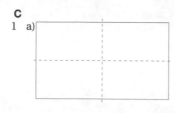

  b) order 2

2
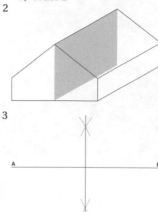

3
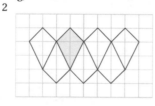

ANGLES

A
1 a
2 c
3 b
4 b
5 a

B
1 a) n = 65°
  b) n = 63°
  c) n = 148°
  d) n = 68°
  e) n = 91°
  f) n = 60°
  g) n = 154°

2

C
1 a) i) x = 18°
    ii) If AB is vertical and BD is horizontal ABE = 90°. So angle x must be 18°.
  b) i) y = 54°
    ii) Triangle BCD is isosceles so angle BDC and BCD are equal hence y must be 54°.
  c) i) z = 54°
    ii) Angle z is an alternate angle with angle BDC since CF and BE are parallel.
2 Sum of interior angles in a hexagon (2n – 4) × 90°. Sum of angles in a hexagon is 720°. Angle x = 105°

BEARINGS AND SCALE DRAWINGS

A
1 c
2 a
3 d
4 b

B
1 10 km
2 a)

  b) 11.1 cm = 22.2 km
  c) 100°
3 false, it is 240°

C
1 a) i) 325 m
    ii) 060°
    iii) 120°
  b)

2 Lengths must be ± 2 mm.

TRANSFORMATIONS 1

A
1 a
2 c
3 b
4 b

B
1

2 a) translation
  b) rotation
  c) translation
  d) reflection

C
1 a) reflection in the x axis.
  b) rotation 90° anticlockwise about (0, 0)

2

TRANSFORMATIONS 2

A
1 d
2 b
3 b

B
1
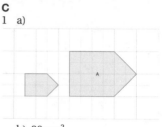

2 a) reflection in the y axis.
  b) rotation 90° clockwise about (0, 0).
  c) reflection in the line y = x

C
1 a)
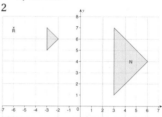

  b) 20 cm²

2

SIMILARITY

A
1 c
2 b
3 b
4 b

B
1 a) true
  b) false
2 a) n = 7.5 cm
  b) n = 6.5 cm
  c) n = 6.5 cm (1 d.p.)
  d) n = 7.3 cm

C
1 The two triangles are similar because the ratio of the sides are the same.
  9 ÷ 7 = 1.2857 .... which is the same as 5.4 ÷ 4.2 = 1.2857.
2 a) i) XM̂N = 83°
    ii) XN̂M = XẐY = 68°
    Angles in a triangle add up to 180°. Therefore 180° – 68° – 29° = 83°
  b) 3.65 cm
  c) 11.74 cm

LOCI AND COORDINATES IN 3D

A
1 c
2 d
3 a
4 d
5 b

B

1

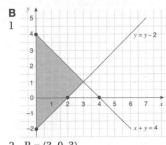

2 R = (3, 0, 3)
S = (3, 3, 1)
T = (0, 3, 1)
U = (0, 1, 1)

C

1

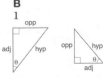

PYTHAGORAS' THEOREM

A
1 d
2 b
3 a
4 c

B
1 a) n = 15 cm
  b) n = 12.6 cm
  c) n = 15.1 cm
  d) n = 24.6 cm
2 Since
  $12^2 + 5^2 = 13^2$
  144 + 25 = 169
  the triangle must be
  right-angled for Pythagoras'
  Theorem to be applied.
3 Both statements are true.
  Length of line = $\sqrt{(6^2 + 3^2)}$
    = $\sqrt{45}$ in surd form.
  midpoint = $\frac{(2 + 5)}{2}$, $\frac{(11 + 5)}{2}$
  = (3.5, 8)

C
1 $\sqrt{61}$ cm
2 24.1 cm
3 13.7 cm
4 $\sqrt{41}$ cm

TRIGONOMETRY 1

A
1 a
2 b
3 d
4 a
5 c

B
1

2 a) n = 5 cm
  b) n = 6.3 cm
  c) n = 13.8 cm
  d) n = 14.9 cm
  e) n = 6.7 cm

---

3 a) 38.7°
  b) 52.5°
  c) 23.6°

C
1 15 cm
2 a) 9.9 cm
  b) 65°
3 18 cm

TRIGONOMETRY 2

A
1 c
2 a
3 d
4 c
5 b

B
1 068°
2 11.5 m (1d.p.)
3 13.8 cm (1d.p.)

C
1 a) 64 km
  b) 73 km
  c) 141°
2 30.1°

ANGLE PROPERTIES OF CIRCLES

A
1 c
2 a
3 d
4 a
5 c

B
1 a) a = 65°
  b) a = 18°
  c) a = 60°
  d) a = 50°
  e) a = 82°
2 John is correct. Angle a is 42°
  because angles in the same
  segment are equal.

C
1 a) 66°
  b) The angle at the centre
    is twice that of the
    circumference. Hence
    132° ÷ 2 = 66°
2 a) <ROQ = 140°
  b) <PRQ = 70°

MEASURES AND MEASUREMENT

A
1 b
2 d
3 a
4 d
5 c

B
1 a) 8000 m
  b) 3.25 kg
  c) 7000 kg
  d) 0.52 m
  e) 2700 ml
  f) 0.00262 km
2 12.5 miles
3 1.32 pounds
4 Lower limit = 46.5 m
  Upper limit = 47.5 m
5 53.3 mph
6 0.1 g/cm³

C
1 a) 17.6 pounds
  b) 48 kilometres
2 80 kg

---

3 a) 1 hour 36 minutes
  b) Average speed 4.4 km/h
4 Length = 12.05 cm
  Width = 5.5 cm

AREA OF 2D SHAPES

A
1 c
2 d
3 b
4 d
5 b

B
1 a) false
  b) true
  c) true
  d) false
2 38.6 cm
3 84.21 cm²

C
1 81 cm²
2 38.8 cm
3 16 cm (to nearest cm)
4 120.24 cm²

VOLUME OF 3D SHAPES

A
1 a
2 c
3 a
4 c
5 d

B
1 Emily is not correct. The
  correct volume is 345.6 ÷ 2
  i.e. 172.8 m³.
2 Volume – 170.2 m³
3 Height = 9.9 cm
4 Volume needs three
  dimensions.
  V – $4r^3$ is only two-
  dimensional, hence must
  be a formula for area and
  not volume.

C
1 64 cm³
2 a) 672 cm³
  b) 0.000672 m³
3 3.2 cm
4 $4r^2p$ volume
  $3\pi \sqrt{(r^2 + p^2)}$ length
  $\frac{4\pi r^2}{3p}$ length
5 3807 cm³

HANDLING DATA
COLLECTING DATA

A
1 b
2 d
3 a
4 b

B
1
type of book	tally	frequency

2 The tick boxes overlap. Which
  box would somebody who
  did 2 hours of homework
  tick? It needs an extra box
  with 5 or more hours.
  How much time do you
  spend to the nearest hour,

---

doing homework each night?
0 up to 1 hour
1 up to 2 hours
2 up to 3 hours
4 up to 5 hours
5 hours and over

3 She is asking only men and
  not both men and women.
  She is also asking men who
  are interested in football as
  they are going to a football
  match, so her results will be
  biased.

C
1
Colour of vehicles	tally	frequency

2 From the list below tick your
  favourite chocolate bar.
  Mars ☐   Twix ☐
  Toblerone ☐ Galaxy ☐
  Bounty ☐   Snickers ☐
  other ....
3 The key to this question is to
  break the question into
  subgroups.
  a) On average how many
    hours per school day do
    you watch television?
    0 up to 1 hour ☐
    1 up to 2 hours ☐
    2 up to 3 hours ☐
    3 up to 4 hours ☐
    Over 4 hours ☐
  b) On average, how many
    hours at the weekend do
    you watch television?
    0 up to 2 hours ☐
    2 up to 4 hours ☐
    4 up to 6 hours ☐
    6 up to 8 hours ☐
    Over 8 hours ☐

REPRESENTING DATA

A
1 d
2 c
3 a
4 b

B
1

Pie chart with segments: Beef (105°), Cheese & Onion (105°), Smokey Bacon (15°), Salt & Vinegar

2
Day	1	2	3	4	5	6	7
Hours of sunshine	3	4	1.5	1	1	3	1.5

C
1 a) 390
  b) 390 + (150 × 10p)
    + (270 × 50p) + (90 × 20p)
    + (180 × 5p)
    total £567

2

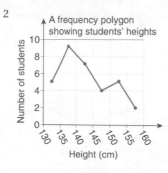

A frequency polygon showing students' heights

SCATTER DIAGRAMS AND CORRELATION

A
1 c
2 a
3 b

B
1 a) Positive correlation
  b) Negative correlation
  c) Positive correlation
  d) No correlation

2 a) Positive correlation
  b)

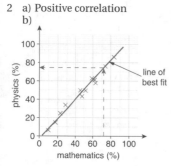

line of best fit

  c) 74% approximately

C
1 a)

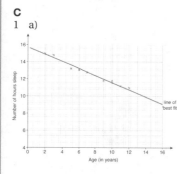

line of 'best fit'

  b) Negative Correlation – the younger the child the more hours sleep they needed.
  c) Line of best fit on diagram above.
  d) A four-year-old child needs approximately 14 hours sleep.
  e) This only gives an estimate as it follows the trend of the data. Similarly, if you continued the line it would assume that you may eventually need no hours sleep at a certain age, which is not the case.

AVERAGES 1

A
1 c
2 b
3 d
4 d
5 b

B

1 a) false
  b) true
  c) false
  d) true
2 a) mean = 141.35
  b) The manufacturer is justified in making this claim since the mean is nearly 142, the mode and median are also approximately 142.
3 $x = 17$

C

1 4.65
2 81
3 £440
3 3.3, 4.6, 3.6, 3, 2.3

AVERAGES 2

A
1 c
2 b
3 a
4 a

B
1 21.5 mm
2 a) mode 47
  b) median 35
  c) range 40

C
1

```
1 | 2 4 9 5 7 8 8 5
2 | 2 7 3 5 7 7
3 | 1 6 5 2 8
4 | 1
```

Reordering gives this.

```
1 | 2 4 5 5 7 8 8 9
2 | 2 3 5 7 7 7
3 | 1 2 5 6 8
4 | 1
```

Key 1|2 means 12 minutes
Stem: 10 minutes

2 a) £31.80
  b) This is only an estimate because the midpoint of the data has been used.
  c) $30 \leq x < 40$

CUMULATIVE FREQUENCY GRAPHS

A
1 c
2 d
3 c
4 a

B
1 a)

Examination mark	Frequency	Cumulative frequency
0–10	4	4
11–20	6	10
21–30	11	21
31–40	24	45
41–50	18	63
51–60	7	70
61–70	3	73

  b)

  c) 36.5
  d) 43 – 28 = 15 marks
  e) 45.5

C

1 a)

  b)

Time (nearest minute)	Frequency	Cumulative frequency
120 < t ≤ 140	1	1
140 < t ≤ 160	8	9
160 < t ≤ 180	24	33
180 < t ≤ 200	29	62
200 < t ≤ 220	10	72
220 < t ≤ 240	5	77
240 < t ≤ 260	3	80

  c) i) interquartile range
       = 198 – 169 = 29 minutes
     ii) 80 – 65 = 15 runners

  d)
Lower quartile Median Upper quartile

PROBABILITY 1

A
1 c
2 d
3 c
4 b
5 a

B
1 a) $\frac{2}{11}$
  b) $\frac{2}{11}$
  c) $\frac{3}{11}$
  d) 0
2 0.65
3 a) true
  b) false
  c) false
4 100 students

C

1 a) i) $\frac{5}{20} = \frac{1}{4}$
     ii) $\frac{7}{20}$
  b) $\frac{16}{20} = \frac{4}{5}$
2 a)

	Under 13 years old	13 years and over	Total
Boys	15	27	42
Girls	12	21	33
Total	27	48	75

  b) $\frac{27}{75} = \frac{9}{25}$

3 a) i) 0.35
     ii) 0
  b) 50 red beads

PROBABILITY 2

A
1 c
2 a
3 a
4 d

B
1 a)

		Spinner 1			
		1	2	3	3
Spinner 2	1	2	3	4	4
	2	3	4	5	5
	3	4	5	6	6
	6	7	8	9	9

  b) i) $\frac{4}{16} = \frac{1}{4}$
     ii) $\frac{2}{16} = \frac{1}{8}$
     iii) 0
2 0.09
3 a) $\frac{49}{169}$
  b) $\frac{84}{169}$

C

1 a) $\frac{6}{36} = \frac{1}{6}$

   b) $\frac{4}{36} = \frac{1}{9}$

2 a)

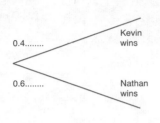

Monopoly

0.4........ Kevin wins

0.6........ Nathan wins

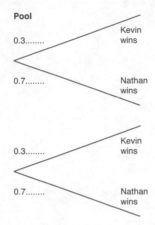

Pool

0.3........ Kevin wins

0.7........ Nathan wins

0.3........ Kevin wins

0.7........ Nathan wins

b) 0.42

LETTS EDUCATIONAL
The Chiswick Centre
414 Chiswick High Road
London W4 5TF
Tel: 020 8996 3333
Fax: 020 8742 8390
Email: mail@lettsed.co.uk
Website: www.letts-education.com